Corruption at Jamestown Prison

By

AJ HUTCHISON

First Edition

Copyright January 2010
AJ Hutchison

Independent Publisher
ISBN 978-1-4507-0344-4

First Printing: January 2010
Arrow Swift Printing
Jackson, Michigan

Authors Note:

This book is fictitious; any description of a person or event that appears to be true is simply coincidence, however, this book is based on some true facts.

Many thanks to Jon Eppley, who edited the entire book, and patiently made notes; also to my family for their moral support and encouragement, especially Bob and Michele for their helpful suggestions and thoughts.

Chapter 1

Over two decades have passed since my home was broken into and my daily-recorded journal was stolen. My notes could be incriminating to those who lived a charade of being righteous, as they were involved in foul play. In some cases their acts were so horrendous that if caught, they could spend time in the penitentiary.

"There she is".

"Harumph!"

It was my first day back to work after being off on sick leave. A very long sick leave; I had a nervous break down. Waiting for roll call I heard someone say, "Welcome back sucker," another voice said, "She has nothin' coming". Then another; "She better play ball". My back stiffened and I went to my assignment.

Later, as I approached an area on the bulkhead where there was a blind spot from the gun turret I heard. ".. Play ball. ...Okay boys, grab her! We'll make a final example. Women do not belong here".
I glanced in the direction of the voices and saw the glimmer of a five-inch shank (home-made knife) raised and slammed into my chest. As I turned to protect myself I felt the second shank enter my side.
"*Run for help*", I thought raising my hands to protect the vital spots, my heart, jugular vein, throat.
I turned to run and a third shank was stabbed into my back.
"Arughhhhhhhhhhhhhh!"

Thank God, I'm awake. Will the nightmares ever end? Over and over, never the same but with the same fear running in my veins and leaving my heart beating so hard it leads to hands shaking and shortness of breath. I thank the Lord who has helped me through these past two decades. Yes, over twenty years!

I know now, that it is time to sit down and put this on paper; all the horrors, life threats, fears and documented corruption that went on in the largest walled prison in the world.
Yes, it is time, for just a few days ago I read that our State government was in the process of closing that prison down. The reasons? Lead

pipes? Not enough taxes to run it? No, there were many reasons, too many experiences just like mine. Reasons that lead to too many lawsuits, too great a turnover of personnel, too many deaths, death attempts, and harassment of a very extreme state.

My story began in the late 1980's, when I was laid off, and couldn't find a job good enough to pay the mortgage and keep food on the table. Also, my husband had left me six months before, having a desire to see the world. I was attending college at the time, and switched my major to Criminal Justice: a pre-requisite for getting a job with the Corrections Department.

Not like in the old days when the officers were called turnkeys, who just came off the farm without any knowledge of the laws, etc. The turnkeys of old were men who beat the prisoners into submission, which was common in most prisons at that time.
The prisoners soon learned that they had rights. Their families found lawyers, and soon the State was being sued for what they called 'over kill'. In reality it meant that the system was guilty of extreme cruelty and using excessive force to control the prisoners.
Indeed, that was just the case when a prisoner was stopped for a strip search. He did not want to be searched in front of a female officer. Fighting against the group of officers holding him down, the prisoner choked to death for lack of air. The prisoner struggled with the officers, kicking a thrashing around his cell. Finally one officer held the prisoner's head against the edge of the bed, while the other three held the remaining parts of the prisoner down. It seemed a long time, but in just a few seconds the prisoner was dead.
I personally believed this was an accidental death, however the prisoner's family looked at the horrific event as excessive force.

In the Criminal Justice courses, I learned about the older types of prison reform, laws, report writing, and procedures. The judicial system was another subject I studied.
No more lawsuits because of uneducated prison guards.
The 'new wave' began after a lawsuit over a prisoner being killed; the mismanagement of guards clinched the decision to make new laws and forms of discipline.
The prisoner refused to submit to a shake down, and was rushed by five guards. When they came off him he was dead. He had strangled, his wind shut off under the pressure on the edge of the cement bed base. The black male prisoner merely did not want a red-haired white

female strip-searching him. The event also caused a change to be made in the process of doing strip-searches. Women officers in the men's prison were alien to the prisoners. And in many cases women were alien to their male co-workers.

So there I was studying and really enjoying a new range of knowledge, passing with high grades, graduating; and finally just waiting. I graduated in April; it was now fall. I waited for the telephone call to work, or an interview, or whatever it takes to 'get the job'.

I received a post card in the mail with an appointment to be interviewed shortly afterwards; the 'shortly' was approximately five months after graduation.

The morning came and sun shined brilliantly on the wet, dewy, fall day. The clock said eight; I had to hurry to be on time for my interview at Brookview High School, a few blocks away from the academy. I quickly showered, dressed, grabbed a slice of toast, and ran out to the car. I was on my way.

The distance from my home to my appointment was approximately 20 miles. This meant it would take around a half-hour to arrive on time.

In the hall were approximately one hundred people, all patiently waiting. I was told we would be called in one at a time to be interviewed.

Finally I heard my name, "Anne Morgan".

Three deputy wardens interviewed me. The one on the end motioned for me to come to his desk. He was the deputy warden, Sam Baldwin, who played volleyball with us at the college graduation picnic. He stood on the opposite of me across the net and witnessed the clash I had with a classmate, looking to see if I was tough enough not to cry. I wonder if he remembered this, I bit it back and smiled.

5

Chapter 2

"So, you are saying, Ms. err, it is Ms. isn't it?"
The 's' buzzed between his teeth. I smiled and nodded as he began again.
"You're saying that you aren't afraid to work in the most dangerous prison in this state, knowing that the first woman hired was brutally murdered just a few short weeks after she was hired?'
The smile that still lingered on my face froze, while a chill went through my whole being. Then looking straight into his eyes I said, "Yes," with a sober, serious expression on my face.

Damn! Damn, damn, damn him, damn the job, and damn me for being so eager to get a good paying job, that I hadn't even watched the news, nor had I heard about this incident, murder, ugh. Damn Ralph for leaving too!

I was too busy trying to prove to everyone else and to myself that I had the courage to do something about my independence, get a job that would help pay for the house that I just bought, and make ends meet.
The Deputy smiled at me and said, "...you'll hear from us in a few weeks, and I don't think you will have any problem being hired."
"Thank you very much, I'll be looking forward to hearing from you, Sir," I said.
As I left I glanced around to see if Diane, a former classmate, was there. Down the hall, towards the entrance, I spotted her.
"Diane, wait up." She turned and acknowledged me.

"I have to ask you something, and by the way, how did you do with your interview?"

"I did fine, and you?" Diane replied.

"Okay. Deputy Baldwin said that I'd be hearing from the Corrections Department very soon. But did you know about that first female officer being killed?"

"Yes. Let's not talk here. Do you have time to go for coffee?"

"Sure, how 'bout I meet you at Rudy's Café, since it's on our way?" I answered.

"Okay, see you there."

It was only 1:25. This gave us time since school let out at three thirty. Diane had three children still in school. The oldest was 14, a girl who was quiet and never spoke to me. The two younger boys were 6 and 8 years old, both usually dressed in matching outfits. They were always smiling.
As I eased the old beater out of the parking lot my thoughts went to Diane. She was tall, at least four inches taller than me, with blond hair that transformed miraculously from blond to a strawberry red hue when the sun fell on it. Blue, blue eyes and an almost pouting mouth, which made one think that she never smiled. I was impressed with her intelligence, because she had a photographic memory. Her husband was great too, with a few minor exceptions not worth mentioning. They had beautiful children one girl, and two boys. Their home is paid for. They seem to be the perfect family.

Diane was there when I arrived.
As I reached the booth, I noticed she had ordered a glass of wine, and a brewsky for me. *'Huh, so much for the coffee'* I thought. The topic called for serious beverages.

"So, tell me about it." I said, sipping my beer, which was unusual for me. I was not a drinker.

"Well, all I really know is what I saw on TV and read in the news. The female officer was assigned to the same location for two weeks, and then the morning of her death, she was assigned to a new location, given a radio, and cold turkey to this new spot. She apparently let a prisoner into her area, which did not belong there. Supposedly he grabbed her, overpowered and raped her. She must have been screaming, so he took his belt, and twisted it around her neck, and squeezed the life out of her. They found a bloody wound on her head. Her radio, with blood on it was nearby. The newspaper had a photo of her and it said something about an estranged husband."

"What does that mean?" I asked.

"Apparently they weren't getting along. I dunno?"

"Well, I need this job. But, have to admit this news turned my blood cold. She shouldn't have been alone. We'll have to really watch ourselves in there."

"Yah, I know. It's scary." Diane looked down at her hands, deep in thought.

We visited a little longer, finished our drinks and left. Driving home, my thoughts went back to what she had told me. It still made me shiver, but I told myself 'you're tough, you can handle it,' and the worried look on my face turned into a smile.
I thought about buying a new car after I knew I had my foot in the door and my finances were stable. It wouldn't take long to save enough for a down payment. All too soon I was turning into my driveway, the twenty- five miles were ate up fast while I dreamed of my financial future.

Chapter 3

About five weeks later, I was hired.
 I spent the better part of the morning in the garden. I was carrying a bushel of ripe tomatoes up to the house to be canned, when I heard the phone ring.

"Hello?" I answered.

"Is this Anne Morgan?"

"Yes, it is."

"This is Deputy Warden Jones from the D.O.C. Since you have passed your civil service exam, and your college courses in Criminal Justice, and meet our criteria, we are asking if you would be willing to work at Jamestown Prison?"
Oh, Lord. The worst choice, if I had one. You need work I reminded myself.
"Yes, this will be fine." I said.

"Okay, report to the Police Academy, Monday September 4th, at 9am, you know where it is, don't you?"

"Yes."

"We will meet at the main building, room 304."

"Thank you, Deputy Jones. I'll be there".

My heart jumped for joy. Work, and paychecks! No more macaroni & cheese, hotdogs, and day-old bread without butter. I immediately called my friend who went through the classes with me. Jumping up and down shouting. 'Hooray! Hooray!'
Ring. Ring. "Hi, Genevieve?"

"Yes."

"Did you get a call from the D.O. C.?"

"Not yet, why?"

"They just called. DW Jones, that is, and asked if I would work at Jamestown Prison."

"You didn't say yes, did you?"

"Yes, you know I need the job, what with Ralph being gone for over a year and all. I'd better hang up in case they're trying to call you. Let me know as soon as you hear."

" I really hope we are hired at the same place. There are so many Prisons opening that it's possible we will be sent in opposite directions," Gen said.
Especially since she lives quite a ways farther west from me, I thought.

"Agreed, I will call as soon as I hear." she said.

"Hi, Diane, have you heard from the DOC?"

"Yes, I've been trying to call you."

"For Jamestown Prison?"

"Next Monday morning at the State Police Academy," she said.

"Oh, okay I'll see you there," I said, "Aren't you excited?"

"Yes and no. It's a dangerous place in there you know."

"Don't remind me, I want to hang on to the joy a little longer. You know, money."
No more than five minutes after I hung up, the phone rang again.

"This is Gen, see you Monday at the academy."

"Jamestown?"

"Yup."

Chapter 4

The Academy is on the northwest part of town. It used to be the municipal orphanage, before it moved. The old campus was converted to a police and corrections academy. There are several buildings, with a cafeteria, housing in the great building and study halls. The new recruits were told that we would get our uniforms the first day. We found out that they were stored in the basement of one of the study halls.

Diane was getting out of her car when I drove into the parking lot. I tooted the horn at her and made a hand signal to wait up for me. It was a good thing I arrived when I did because the parking lot was already three-quarters full and it was only 8:35.

"Hi, Diane. I was wondering if I had called you? I did so many, I've been so busy this weekend that I didn't have time to call you."

"Yes you did call me. This is exciting, isn't it Anne? Just think we are going to be together in training. You know they are hiring in groups. Some of the persons that we studied with haven't been called yet. "

"I am worried about working 'in there,' but it is a job, and it is money."

"That's right, we have to think positive. I'll be working there also. We won't know what shift, or location yet."

"Oh, guess who else will be here this morning. You remember Genevieve from Scotsville?"

"Oh, ya, I do remember her."

We were almost to building 'D', which was the main building. The line was backed up right out the door and down the sidewalk. I overheard someone say that we needed to get papers from personnel, wait until nine o'clock then meet in the main auditorium, room 304. I didn't see Jen anywhere, but this was usual for her she had always pulled up for class just on time.
By the time we had inched our way to the front of the line, received instructions and papers, it was eight forty two, and still no Genevive.

Diane said, " Well, this will give me time for one more cigarette before we go over to the auditorium. Damn that Jen. Where is she?"

I looked again towards the parking lot; she was just pulling in with her white Monte Carlo.

"Here she comes, now," I said.

"I had a flat tire the first day. I can't believe it!" Jen called to us.

"Well, hurry and get your papers in this building. We'll wait," I said.

When she came back out, she was smiling and said it was going to be all right. They excused her tardiness.

We all gathered in the auditorium, found a seat and waited. At precisely nine, the principal of the academy, James E. Jones welcomed each and every one. Next, Superintendent Mr. Harold Herschberger introduced the Director of the Department of Corrections, Malcolm Fairchild. He said a mouth full of nothing and concluded by saying, 'be careful in there.'

After the welcome and presentation, we filled out our W-2's and other employment papers, including life insurance papers, (like 'in case of death' papers). If I were killed in the line of duty my benefactor would receive $250,000.

Our rooms were assigned to those who were going to stay main building of the Academy; Genevieve definitely was not going to stay there!

"I'll drive to and fro; it's not that far!"

Well it was that far, she was way out west of town over thirty-five miles. *Darn, I wanted her to be my 'roomie.'* So, meet new people and broaden my acquaintances.

I was still thinking about whom I would have to room with, whether I wanted to share with someone. As I walked to the study hall I decided that it would be okay. It was only a few weeks, and then we were into the system, working at our designated prisons.

We met again in the study hall, and were instructed to read the information about our physical education course and requirements in order to pass on to the actual job.

We were each required to run a mile in 15 minutes or less, do 16 pushups in 10 seconds, 20 sit-ups in 15 seconds and be able to climb 'big bertha' up and back continuously for nine minutes.

What? There is more to this than I thought! Okay. And the bell rang for lunch. We were instructed to resume again in front of the study hall at 1pm.

Our class was large enough to divide it into three platoons for drills. There were 90 men and six women. Two of the women were black, each from a larger city. Of the 96 recruits only some would end up with us at Johnstown.

One of the new recruits name was Peggy Cook. Diane, Jen and I decided to name her Copper Penny, because her hair was the color of a penny. Peggy was a bit of a loner, and I knew she would be hard to get to know, right off. I can't remember the fifth woman's name. She was assigned to the regional prison in the northeastern part of the state, and I never saw her again after we left the Academy.

Ms. Watson, the sixth, was assigned to my room. She wore a jet-black wig; her skin was very dark, and to describe her she had a sense of humor that wouldn't quit. She stood about five three, called everyone 'others' and would continue laughing until we joined in with her. I never did know her first name; she went to a camp up north. When she found out where she was going all she said was 'Lordy, Lordy preserve my soul.' Being a big city girl, this was going to be a new frontier for her.

Della Daniels, number five, was a light-skinned Afro-American woman with a mole that accentuated her good looks. She had a full set of teeth that shined white when she smiled, which was often. Della stood five eleven. She had average-length curly hair that was relaxed into a soft curl.

So, as I was saying, there were six women, and ninety men; I guess we were filling in that particular quota of minorities.

The remaining part of the day was filled with excitement for me and I'm sure for the others also.

We were divided into three divisions. One went for P.E.; another group took individual pictures for their laminated State I.D., and the third group was being fitted with our new uniforms and including shoes.

As we finished each procedure we would switch with the previous group until each had finished getting photos, uniforms and physical training.

I found out after running for my mile that the shoes were made by the prisoners and the soles were a fraction of an inch too long, which caused me to trip if I wasn't careful.

By the time the three groups had rotated through each phase it was time to go home or stay at the Main Building if we were from out of town.

My thoughts were on the days experience so far. Our instructors were simply trying to prepare us for the 'inside.' Then there was running the mile, pushups, sit-ups, and big bertha. Big Bertha was the steps; I swear they were over twelve inch high. Two steps up and two back.

Even though we were on the payroll, if we couldn't run the mile in fifteen minutes, and pass the physical, we would be removed from the academy.

We showered and met for dinner at six.

The first day was over; full and continuous, sleep came easily. My 'roomie', Officer Watson was still talking when I fell asleep.

"Hi, Bob! Oops…Officer North, what's happening this morning?"

Bob was ex-military. He said he was a marine pilot before he was rifted, so he could not claim a retirement from the service. He was elected to be one of the drill leaders, so I was impressed with his know how.

"Well, we're to assemble in the same groups that we were in yesterday. From what the Sgt. said, I understand we will be drilling the first hour everyday. We're just waiting 'til eight o'clock," he said.

"Wow! I didn't know that we would be doing drills, this really is military oriented in more than one way."

"Yes, it is. We are to pick a drillmaster from our platoon, and I'd like to suggest Officer Kempf. He was in the Marines, just as I was, and should be good at it."

"It's okay with me," I said. From a distance across the lawn I spotted Diane.

"Oh, here comes Diane…. er, officer Collins, it's too bad she was put in the other platoon," I continued, "Good morning officer Collins, don't you look spiffy in your uniform!"

"As soon as I get used to it." Stretching her neck at the discomfort of the tie.

Genevive and I were the only two from our college group in our platoon, however we were getting to know each other with every passing experience and blunder. Tripping over each other, what a travesty we were. We studied our asses off. We were tested every day on what we were taught, and if you did not have a score of seventy or more, you were all done. Kaput!
Each day we watched to see if one or two packed up and went home. The last hour of each day was devoted to P.E., including situps, push-ups, Bertha. The final test was to run a mile and half in 15 minutes.

Officer Bobby North, the ex-marine pilot, was a suspicious character; he finished all his tests within 5 minutes and left the room, smoked a cigarette, and always passed with flying colors. He told me conflicting stories and apparently forgot what he had said. First he said he was rifted in the Marines, the next story was his wife divorced him and took his retirement money. I believed that he should be watched. I didn't trust him after the first tale.

Six weeks passed so fast. It was hard to believe it was over and next Monday was O.J.T. (on job training) for two weeks. I was delegated to be a group representative helping to solve problems. One in particular was taking O. Watson aside and speaking to her about her tainted language. Many officers were offended. I wonder when the prisoners used mother f**ker, if they were offended. Fortunately, she took it quite well.

Officer Kempf did end up being our drillmaster. He took to me too, but I knew it was short term; he was sent to a prison that was 500 miles away from the one I would be assigned to. He was a cartoonist and drew a picture of what it would be like for the women working in a male prison.

Our platoon did win the drill competition. The class was divided into three platoons, which competed against each other. This took place the last day of the first segment of academic training.
We went inside for two weeks and then back for the final segment of training.

That evening Genevive and I were walking towards the parking lot when we both said simultaneously, ' let's cut our hair! '
"Jinx! Ha Ha!"

"Well, let's do it," Genevive said.

So we did. My hair was near mid-back length. When I left the beauty saloon it was very short and male-ish.
I took a deep breath. Oh well. So was Genevives'. Our short hair, along with our choice to use the male tie instead of the female bowtie was a statement. We wanted to make the prisoners and the male officers realize that we were not pansies.

Chapter 5

Arriving at Jamestown Prison that morning, the world's largest walled prison, brought anticipation of the unknown. What or how will I feel, react? My heart gripped with fear. Stop it, I scolded, I was ushered past the Reception desk, towards the gate. My feet dragged, and time stood still. What am I doing here? Am I ready for this? The pounding in my chest made me giddy. I had reached the first gate. The Officer opened it to let at least 10 through at a time. There were fifteen in my group going through. The barred gate opened. I stepped through with the others as the Officer counted, then held up his hand to stop the next recruit, then signaled to the gate operator using the controls.

The barred gate slammed behind me. There were about a 15 officers in the front gate with me. We were between two gates that were monitored by three officers; two were in the gated areas with us, and the third was behind a bulletproof window. Behind him was another officer in charge of the arsenal. The officer in the window controlled the open and shut buttons, on both gates. Inside lead to the control center, offices and out to the cellblocks. The outside gate leads you to the information desk and to the parking lot where visitors and employees left their vehicles.

"Listen up folks. Empty your pockets, have your State ID ready to be checked by Officer Daniels here, and go one at a time through the metal detector." Said Captain Street.
He was pointing at Officer Daniels. No relation to Della.
When we had all been checked, the inside gate opened, leading us to the Control Center. From there, the group (thirty-six) was ushered to a large room beyond the marble floored control center, where each of us was assigned a training officer.
There were a total of 36 'green' officers starting at Jamestown Prison. We grouped our way through the barred gates into the control center. The Captain on duty came out of his office to address the group.

We were told that customarily, we would come into the control center, have Roll Call, and a briefing of events from the previous shift.
Each day of our O.J.T., we would be assigned to a veteran officer to learn each assignment duties at that specific location. When we came back after graduation from academy, we would be on our

own without the veteran officer. We had three more weeks to finally complete our academy training.

Monday morning, I was assigned to the roof, with Sergeant Romano. He showed me each Gun Post as he did his rounds, signing the logbook and briefing me on any unique details of each post. We walked from gun post to gun post along a flat roof in the shape of a 'U.' There were five cell blocks all connected, divided with heavy yellow brick double thick walls. Each cell housed approximately 450 - 500 inmates.

We spent a larger part of the day in 'The Tank,' which was what they named the gun turret over the dining room. It extended from the east wall to the west wall in order to be able to shoot warning shots when the prisoners were fighting, knifing, or killing. 'The Tank' was made of thick steel sheeting with peek holes throughout it. The one opening in the center was eight inches by twenty-four, which was the largest. The view was a good vantage point, over-looking the entire dining room, which held approximately 1,000 inmates at one time. The only time it was necessary to move to another peek hole was to observe the movement in the kitchen and bakery.

Sergeant Romano was an elderly Italian man with dark, curly hair, streaked with silver and gray. He was professional, and did his job meticulously; never once did he ask personal questions. He was impressive yet had a congenial demeanor.

I went home thinking that this could be easier than I expected.

The next day I was assigned to the gun turret on the north side of the prison. It was there to monitor two cellblocks. I had to walk continuously from one peephole to another during mass movement. This was when the 'incidents' could happen.

My partner Officer Jarvis told me about a female officer that had mistakenly left her radio on while she was making out with her partner. Everyone who had a radio, the Control Center, the Arsenal, the entire prison could hear it. *What's his game,* I thought*? Do I act like one of the guys and just laugh it off?*

He continued his narration," Honcha, honcha, honcha....".

Creep, this wasn't necessary.

I shrugged my shoulders and walked over to the other side for a while. When I came back I made sure I remained professional, and avoided letting the conversation go in that direction again.

Day-three was something new. I was assigned to one of the checkpoint gates with a tiny, blond-haired, female officer. I signed the log, and spent the day making sure that a prisoner coming or going had a pass.

Her horror story was that she was in the auditorium when the prisoners rushed her during movie night. If it weren't for one, very tall, strong, black prisoner, she would have been hurt. *This told me that you could 'trust' a prisoner?* I asked myself.

Thursday morning, my assignment was with officer George Harvey. I knew him from my Aikido training the week before. Aikido was a form of self-defense, which was a part of the training program. Officer Harvey was the instructor.

Harvey was impressive with his muscular build, and arrogant ways. There was no doubt that he could handle himself, if he was caught in a situation.

Our assignment included the college rooms, library on second floor, more classrooms on first, also the stage, balcony, and auditorium, (where my blond officer from the day before had her scare,) some storage rooms backstage, and the foyer entrance where we were supposed to be during mass movement. There was a door on the east side of the stage.

"Where does that door lead to?" I asked.

"Oh, that's just to the storage room and extra supplies. It's never used," he said, looking me in the eyes, "You know about the female officer being killed? Well, this is where it happened."

"Where?"

"I'll show you." He used his pass key and opened the west door to the stage, pointed to a spot and said, " This is where it started he must have dragged her down the steps to this enclosed area leading to the auditorium, 'cause that is where they found her."

Shivers ran up my spine. "So what's your story?" I asked.

"All I know is hearsay; that she was assigned to this area, she was the only officer in the building, and that she let a prisoner in to get supplies he needed from the storage room off the stage. The news said 'She was approached by a prisoner, who said he needed some supplies from a closet,' something like that. 'She let him in and he killed her.'"

We walked halfway up through the auditorium to an opening that returned to the classrooms. In it's dark alcove, he grabbed me and kissed me!

Was this playing ball? They said she didn't play ball and that's why she was killed. Just respond. Think straight. No whys, no questions, just act normal. After all, you need this job. You are not dead and you aren't going to be.

He continued on to show me the remaining rooms in the school and then we wove our way back, through the dark alcove, into the dark auditorium. There were some dim lights gleaming from the two story high ceiling.

Just as we went up the stage steps, all at once the entire building was in darkness. I had reached the top of the steps ahead of him. I was standing precisely on the spot where Mayberry had been killed!

"Don't move!" He said, from behind me.

The h--- you say, looking around for some light at all. Walking in the direction of the exit door, I could see a small dim light coming from the six-by eight-inch window. I reached to my key clip, my hands shaking so hard I couldn't control them. I could hear his footsteps coming from behind me, I could hear his breathing. My hands shaking, reaching for the doorknob, and the key lock directly below.
Be calm. Use both hands.
There it is, guide it in with both hands.
Both hands still shaking, there, it's in.
Turn the key, ah! At last the door is open.
Dark here too!
What's happening?
Officer Harvey was directly behind me, within a few steps. Walking directly to the entrance door, using my passkey again, not stopping for anything or anyone, until I was out of the building.

"Hey, you were great! You passed the test in my book. I'll work with you anytime", he said.

There was shouting form the control center's loud speaker, "Remain at your assignment! There is a power outage. The back up generator should have all lights on shortly."

You SOB I thought, still shaking, I really thought he did this on purpose. Then when it was dark throughout the entire building, I wondered. Passed the test, eh? What did he mean by that? Of course he would work with me anytime. I did everything, as he wanted. Even let him kiss me.

I looked at him and very calmly said, "Thank you."

The next day I was assigned to Sergeant Robinson, a short, stocky, young, black man, with a round kind face, who was the Sergeant for 'C' block. I remained by him at the desk and hang with the base officer, just to get some experience with close contact in the block, face to face with the prisoners.
Each block consisted of two sides with five galleries each. Namely base, first, second, third, and fourth gallery, housing approximately fifty prisoners on each gallery. So there were approximately two hundred fifty per side and five hundred residents per block.
I was with officer Flatland down base about halfway from the Sergeant's desk, when I heard the phone ring. I knew he would answer it, so I didn't. He said something, briefly, and glanced my way, set the phone down and called to me. I approached the desk area as fast as I could. Stepping out of the glassed-in office, he said in a low voice, "The call is for you, it's officer Harvey. This is just a word for the wise, stay away from him. He's trouble."

Oh, boy. I looked into his kind eyes and knew he was trying to tell me something, but I would have to figure it out for myself. I decided Harvey was trouble, but hearing it made me more sure about my hunch.

By this time it was Friday evening, the first week of O.J.T. was complete. I looked at the clock and was glad that the shift was over.
Driving home that evening, I thought about the day. How Robinson warned me, how Harvey wanted to take me out to lunch someday soon, how I would have to put him off for now. My thoughts wandered to the previous day. How my hands shook so hard, fear clutching my heart.
The only other time in my life that my hands shook hard was once when my husband and I went ice fishing up north near Sarawak floodwaters.
The landlord had cut the openings in the ice, in expectations for the New Years Holiday fishermen. I was in my shanty alone, fire keeping

me warm, almost drowsy. I hooked a shiner on a fishing line and attached the lure to a nail on the two-by-four; leaving the shiner to swim around in the water. Bending over watching through the 14 by 22 inch opening in the ice, when all at once the biggest walleye I had ever seen shot into view, swallowed my shiner, hook and all. I grabbed the taunt line, my hands were shaking as I brought a 26 inch fish out of the ice, slapping all over on the wooden floor of the shanty.

My hands were shaking three times as worse yesterday in the auditorium of the Education Building. I chuckled nervously to myself, as I heaved a sigh of relief. Everything is okay. I am alive, and I am not dead. But I will never forget.
That night I prayed that nothing would happen to me or any other female officer again.
Monday of the second week I was assigned to the gate near the infirmary. This was an easy shift. The week went on with new assignments; each day passing quickly without memorable incidents.

The first day back at the academy, we were instructed where we would work, and on what shift. Second shift was okay with me. Afternoon shift would enable me to get my chores at home done before leaving for work. I had a garden and a large lawn, in fact almost two acres.
 However, I felt disappointed because Diane would be working day shift, in 'B' Block, where I would hardly see her, just on days off. Della Daniels was in custody with me, so we would be able to talk sometimes. Jen was assigned to Protective Custody (P.C.), where all the 'sissies' and 'snitches' were housed.

There we were back at the Academy for the final three weeks. So far, we had done some serious learning. Our instructor told us about how prisoners could use us in a set-up; one would distract you with conversation, while another one or more would break the rules without our knowing it. All the prisoners had was time they would spend it making plans, and seeing which officer could be easily distracted.
We learned that instead of using force as a means to control the prisoners, we should write them up. This deterrent would be loss of privileges, such as no library, put their TV in storage for a certain amount of time, job removed, no yard for a week. If the infarction is serious enough they would be sent to administrative segregation, (Ad Seg) One of the most serious offense was when the officer found

contraband in the prisoners cell. Being out of place was a more serious write up. So serious that in many cases it was considered attempted escape. In this case the prisoner would be placed in Administrative Segregation.
When a prisoner was sent there, he would be cuffed each time he left his cell. When in the showers, the prisoner would back up to the open slot and have the Officer un-cuff him.
When Ad. Seg. prisoners had yard, the same process would take place; the prisoner was cuffed and only un-cuffed when he was locked in a separate yard cage. Each cage had a telephone, where the prisoner could call home, if the family member was willing to accept charges.

    The final three weeks of academy were dedicated to physical education, making sure we were in shape to pass the Phys Ed test. Without passing we would be without a job.
We saw the film "Brubaker," with Robert Redford, and "Scared Stiff," which gave us more familiarity with prison life.
I believe that the closest movie picture that reveals how it is inside the prison is the one with Tom Seleck named "An Innocent Man," I viewed this movie long after working 'inside'.
Most of all, we did drills, drills, and drill, to prepare us for our competition. The competition was between three platoons, which was a part of the final, at the upcoming graduation. This taught us discipline also, and kept us in shape for the upcoming job.
It seemed that those three weeks flew by so fast. One morning, as we arrived at class, we saw the flag was flying at half-mast.
Sgt. Brown began by saying, "One of the officers was killed at Jamestown. It was during mass movement. He had released his gallery and was walking casually with the 50 residents as they were leaving the gallery. Somehow, as he passed three prisoners, one shoved a shank into his heart. It happened so fast; there was no way to save him. He bled to death right there before the eyes of his fellow workers. Total lock-down took place immediately. Sirens were blowing and "Big Red" was shot off from the gun turret, but no one saw who did it."
Sgt. Brown hung his head, a sad expression on his face as he completed his narration. He paused, collected his thoughts, looked up and said, "There is no way that we can prepare you for this. We can teach you everything about the laws, the rules, control, and deterrents, but when it comes right down to each situation you will have to make a judgment call, it will be up to you, and you alone."

Then the Sergeant said, "Questions? Let's have an open discussion."
The questions came like bullets from a machine gun. I didn't want any part of the discussion. I knew that what the instructor said was enough and the truth. We needed hands-on experience to know exactly what to do in any given situation.
I came out of my daydream when I heard the Sgt. Brown say that we would close for lunch and meet back at the parking lot at one o'clock, where there would be a bus waiting to take us to the gun range.
The bus ride was a short ride just north of the airport. When we arrived, there were instructors from the State Police and Corrections Department to assist us and give direction.
First we learned how to load and shoot a .223 bolt-action rifle, 10 shells to a clip. It was necessary to get a score of 75 or better in three targets. I stood back and let the others shoot, because this was a first for me. I would take my turn when they asked me. Watching the others was very educational. Holding the rifle correctly, then aiming, holding one's breath, and pulling with carry through so as not to jerk. I heard words like 'figure-eight.' To 'carry through' meant to pull the trigger all the way back. Never jerk it; your shot would go up in the air.
It was my turn. All the directions came through my mind. Aim, hold your breath, and mentally count to ten. If you haven't shot by then, start over. I loved it! It came naturally to me, and I qualified in the first two targets! I thanked God, for without Him I could not have done it. I considered myself a very contented person. No one hollered at me, nor made me feel incompetent, as was true of the remaining officers. The instructors were great!
Next we went to the back of the building where there were two 50-gallon barrels. We learned to load and shoot the shotgun. Also, we learned the parts of the shotgun, which we would be tested on later. It was a Remington 870 pump action shotgun, the parts were butt plate, stock, receiver, safety, trigger, trigger guard, breech block, slide guard, loading port, ejection port, chamber, magazine release, barrel, fore end, knurl nut, front sight and muzzle. The five-point safety check was 1. Check safety, 2. Check Magazine- push loading port, 3. Check chamber - push slide release button (open one inch). 4. Make sure knurl nut is tight, and 5. Check safety. Always remember four-in-the-chamber if it is full. We were told about Big Red, too. This was a warning shot that just made truly a BIG NOISE. We were directed to shoot Big Red first, as a warning, and then shoot live ammo when necessary.

One black, male recruit was having difficulty. His eyesight was very poor, and he really needed glasses. He did so well with his tests scores, but after his third try for a 70 or better score with the rifle, and a lot of patience from the instructor, he was informed that he didn't pass. This was hard on him, I could see the disappointment in his eyes, yet the kindness from the instructor showed when he said that he should get corrective glasses and re-apply for the job. It wasn't a closed door.

The option to shoot the pistol was up to each individual officer, and not required to be able to work. Of course, I wanted to see if I could handle it. Shooting a pistol was a challenge to me. I have small hands; the butt of the Smith & Weston 38 revolver was big and clumsy for me.

The instructor was saying, "I will blow the whistle, you are being timed; when I blow it again you stop shooting."

"Ready on the right, ready on the left, commence shooting." Wheeeeeeeeeet! The whistle went.

There were several moves and maneuvers to complete shooting; standing, sitting, squatting, right handed, left handed, leaning against a prop, and just holding the pistol in front of you.

It took several attempts, but I mastered it. This was another thankful time between me, and the Man upstairs.

The following is an example of the type of assignments I had in the Academy. This particular one was on Racism. I wrote it as though it was my experience, but I was told about it from a friend. When I was given the marked paper back from the instructor he had written this note on the top:

Instructor's comments:
This paper is excellent, thanks for sharing. You seem to have a good insight into human behavior. The example you use is so true of racisms. Good Work. I think you will be a good Correctional Officer, keep up the good work. Sgt. Brown
Score 4.0
Assignment on Racism
Sgt. Brown's Class,
Score 4.0.

CURFEW

'It was a little past nine on an evening in July of 1967. A curfew had been set for all residents in the city, to be off the streets by nine o'clock.

My father and I were sitting on the front porch talking to a young national guardsman. There were an extra amount of guards in our area, because of the highly inflammable chemical tanks across the street from where I lived.

As I sat there half listening to my father and the guardsman talking, I heard a car in the distance. It started up, and after a few moments it stopped. Within two minutes I heard excruciating screams. My vision, of two hundred yards away by the railroad tracks, was about a two-inch gap, between obstacles. I could see a person running, on fire. The eleven o'clock news revealed that a black Baptist Minister, who was out after nine, was accosted by a mob of militant white youths. They battered him, poured gas on him and set him on fire. He died four days later.   The events that led to this unfortunate deed took place a few days earlier, when a rookie cop had decided to raid a strip on 12th and Pingree Ave. It was an area that had a history of blind pigs, pimps, hookers, and the lot: ordinarily keeping their business going until four or five in the morning. Prior to the raid, it was common knowledge by many that the police ignored these activities, being rewarded with a certain amount of consideration.

The raid caused rioting to break out in various areas throughout the city. The mayor appealed to the Governor for help from the National Guard, since the rioting was getting out of hand. Originally starting out as a racial issue, it had turned into a mass free-for-all.   Three days after the death of the Baptist Minister, a funeral was held at the little church, on the corner of Field and Strong. The news showed that Martin Luther King and another young Baptist Minister, Jesse Jackson, were present.

That little Baptist Church grew in size and notoriety, although the scars of these events still remain. Many parts of the city have never, to this day, re-built that which was destroyed.'

I was grateful to a friend who had narrated the true facts of the events in my paper. He lived in Detroit when the riots took place. His name was Joe Van Den Weingartz. Joe was the one that convinced me to try for a state job. I was working part-time at a convenience store where he would stop and get gas on his way to work.
"Hi, Joe, on your way to work?" I asked. He was dressed in his state uniform, being an officer at the local prison. Before long he would

take time to talk about his past. He had lived with his father in Detroit before he moved back east to be near his mother. She was failing, and needed him.

"Yes, I have day shift this week," he answered. "You'll be done with classes soon, won't you?"

"Yes, I'm in racial discrimination class right now," I told him.

That was when he told me about the evening in Detroit. I remembered each event as he related his experience to me. When I wrote the paper on racisms, I used his exact words as I recalled them.

The last class taken before we went into our first day of work was on a Saturday. It was called 'Inter-personal Communications'. And what it really meant was; 'you are saying this, but what you really mean is that.' We went thorough different scenarios and worked them out, tested and the day was over. Graduation was on Friday of the following week.

Chapter 6

The job began on a cold day in January. Being hired in late October we spent 6 weeks of academy and 2 weeks of on the job training. Graduation was held just before Christmas, leaving a week off before returning to work in the new-year. My uniform included slacks, shirt, tie, blazer, winter coat with a zip out lining, a fur lined cap that flipped down over my ears, and a pair of leather black shoes.

My first day went without incident. Soon the weeks were flying by and things became routine. Two days on the ground and three on the roof. Being a good shot gave me this position as well as incidental trips as transporting a prisoner to the hospital or another prison. I was assigned to Security. The other division was called Housing.

Everything became routine. One day my radio barked out an order, "Officer Morgan, report to the control center". My Sergeant sent my relief and away I went.

"Go to the Arsenal, get a Pistol and go with Officer Cook to the prison hospital, you know where it is located, over in the north end of the complex, not the infirmary. I need you to escort a prisoner to the hospital downtown. Take a state car; the officer in the Arsenal has the keys."

"Yes Captain Wiggins, thank you."

I'll never forget this partner; I privately called him Officer Gook after that day. Primarily, because he was not pistol qualified, so I wore mine, as protection in case something happened.

When we arrived at the prison hospital, the male nurse said that the prisoner had slipped in the kitchen when he was helping prepare the night dinner. He supposedly hurt his back. The ambulance had been called from the hospital downtown, so we waited until it arrived.

I took Officer Cook aside.

"Cook, you will be driving the state car, following the ambulance." I told him. He was green, had been working only a couple months.

"Why? Why are you riding in the ambulance?" he asked.

Oh, brother, I thought, *where did they find this guy?*

"Security," I told him. "If he tries to escape, I have the gun."

"Oh." His mouth hung there open in a perfect zero. *Like his brain,* I thought.

Arriving at the hospital, we were ushered into a room in emergency. I stayed in the room; Officer Cook hung in the hall, and partly in the room while we waited for a doctor to see prisoner Buchanan. He was strapped to a gurney, although his arms were free, moaning in pain. The nurse had directed the EMT to lay the gurney on a stretcher in the emergency room. A nurse returned and said that prisoner Buchanan needed an x-ray. The technician would be there shortly. As she left the room prisoner Buchanan raised his head, and asked me to give him a magazine to read.

Thought he was supposed to lay flat until they knew how bad he was damaged.

Alert, alert, what's wrong with this picture? How could he possibly hold a magazine if he is injured? My doubts were rising.

Next thing I know, Officer Cook was talking to two men, who appeared to be visitors, because they had on long overcoats. They kept looking into the room at the prisoner, and talking nonchalantly to Officer Cook.

What is he doing now? He is an airhead. Doesn't he realize the seriousness of our assignment? I thought.

Buchanan said loudly, "I be goin' to de x-ray room, den I be goin' back to de place."

"Yes, that's right," I answered.

The tech arrived and we wheeled down the hall to the x-ray room. The tech put an apron on me for protection. I stood near, but not out of the room. Officer cook stood in the hall. The tech took one photo, then removed it and came back for the next one. He nodded his head, like a come-here nod. I moved closer to him and he whispered, "There's nothing wrong with him, I just want you to know this."

"Okay, thanks." *I figured as much, when he lifted his head without pain in the waiting room.*

Officer Cook and I waited for the doctor to read the x-rays. After a few minutes, which seemed like hours, the doctor said that prisoner Buchanan was fine, and that we could return to the prison. I called to let the shift commander know that prisoner Buchanan's back was okay; we were leaving, and would be back shortly. I told him what had taken place in the hall with the two men, and prisoner Buchanan's yelling out to them?

"Do you need back up?" the Captain said.

"No, I believe we can handle it, sir."

" Keep your eyes open," he warned.

"Yes sir, see you when we have him back in the block."

I sent Officer Cook out ahead with the gurney. Placing it in the trunk, he came around and unlocked the State car. He looked back at me and nodded.
I ordered the prisoner to advance towards the car from the emergency room door.
Within seconds we were off the sidewalk and headed to the car across the wide drive. A large dark Cadillac car slowly crept towards us with parking lights on. I recognized the same two men who were talking to Officer Cook in the hall. I flipped the strap off the pistol holster, and held it ready if necessary. Heart thumping in my chest, I vowed to use it if I had to. Closer and closer the car crept at a snails pace towards us. Prisoner Buchanan, who was walking just ahead of me, had an arrogant demeanor, and was chuckling to himself. I kept walking and held my hand on the pistol butt, ready.
The car stopped. I looked straight into the eyes of the driver, for a few seconds he sat there, then shoved the pedal down and screeched out of the hospital driveway. Buchanan lost his arrogant attitude and threw himself into the back seat. He wore a dark expression, and remained silent all the way back to the prison.
This could have been an attempt to escape, but it didn't work. Apparently they didn't have a guns, and didn't want to get shot over an attempt to help Buchanan escape. At any length, it didn't happen.
Arriving back at the prison, Officer Cook and I took the prisoner back to his lock in. Removed his cuffs and let the base officer take him to his cell.
We reported everything to the shift commander, Captain Wiggins.
He shook his head and said, "Well, you did a good job. He is being transferred up state tomorrow morning to 'Snow Country,' in the mountain region. He probably did call his cronies to see if you made a slip-up so they could get him from you."
That's where Officer Kemp went. I thought. We heard that everyone towed the line there. No one wanted to be sent there, and usually this happened when a prisoner had too many tickets written because of behavior, and couldn't be controlled.

"Thanks, Captain. I figured as much." I said.

S—t, thanks a lot. *I could have had a better partner. I never told him what kind of officer Cook was, he would find out sooner or later. I just mentally thanked God for His help.*

It seemed good to be away from 'the zoo' for two whole days. Spending time with my family, getting the yard mowed and groomed. Just sitting under the big old oak tree absorbing the sun. God's glorious Creation took away any memories of my week's encounters. The squirrels scampered here and there, jumping from one branch to another. Birds were chirping, the essence of the flowers in my tiered flower garden made me feel like I was in Heaven.

All too soon the weekend was over and I was on my way back to work. Everything put to the rear of my mind reached out and hit me. Today shouldn't be too difficult; I called ahead and found out that I would be at the bakery gate. Although that was what it was called, it actually was between the storage rooms and on down the hall to the kitchen area. Time passed fast and everything usually went pretty smooth in this location.

One exception was a few months ago when a runner (porter for receiving and guidance center) asked me if I had ever dated a black man. Four days later I found out why he was trying to distract me. He was the 'lookout' for his 'homies.' He talked to me while they stole some peach juice from the storage room and put the juice with lots of sugar in a five-gallon pail to ferment. I smelled it the following week and found it. It was hidden behind a pile of dirty aprons and white uniforms. Prisoners wore uniforms while cooking and serving on the dining room food line. Rather than writing a ticket I just poured it down the drain. Boy, were they mad! We were warned about set-ups at the academy, that was my first, but definitely not the worst nor the last.

The Shift Commander boomed out, "Prisoner School, get your keys and radio. I'm putting officer Smith with you, go easy on him since he's green."

"Yes, sir."

What happened to my assignment on the bakery gate? There must have been a change in assigned location.

My partner for the day, was not only new on the job, he was a real nerd. Do I have the word 'mom' tattooed on my forehead?

Apparently the officer assigned to this position called in sick, and I was assigned there once a week so I fell into that slot.

"Officer Smith, would you like to take the radio and make the rounds? I 'll cover the desk and take the radio back when we leave here to go to the mess hall." I asked.

"Great! You're the first one to let me take one." He gratefully replied.

"Well, don't let me down now. When you are called from the control center, don't forget to answer and let them know we're all right. You know, say 'code four'?"

"Right, right."

"Remember to be cautious in the blind spots, where you could run into something dangerous. Always be aware."

"Yes, officer Morgan, I will remember." Looking at me with an unsure expression.

"All you have to do is take a round each half hour and report back here, I will log it down."

He left humming to himself.

The porter was sweeping the hall and area around my desk, preparing to mop it. I started my first entry in the logbook, which was kept locked in the top desk drawer.

"You know Mam, er...."

"Officer."

"Alright, o'cer, I want to say, you must be careful working in here. I see they gave you a green horn for a partner." He was a tall light skinned Afro-American.

"I think I can handle it."

"Have you worked here before?" he asked.

"I work here weekends."

"Dat's my day off, I guess dat's why I haven't seen you before. You know dat o'cer that be killed here?"

"I heard about it."

"She wadn't killed by one of us, it be o'cers."

"What makes you think that?" I felt a chill.

"I know. I wadn't working here then, but my Bunkie did and he swears it be one or more o'cers."

"Don't be telling the wrong person that, and thanks for the warning," I said.

"You seem like a nice person, so I thought I'd tell you, but you didn't hear it from me."

"Got it."

The dork. What's his angle? Does he want me to think prisoners aren't bad? What does he want? Was it really... an officer or more than one?

32

Why would... did she see something she shouldn't have? Quit it, Anne, you're going to get in an uproar. Calm down, just keep your tongue in your cheek and a smile on your face.

I bent my head and continued logging the day's entry, dismissing the porter and his gossip. He continued his mopping, and glancing my way to see if I would notice.

I didn't.

Chapter 7

The phone rang.
"Hi, Anne, it's Diane."
"Yup, I recognize your voice. What's up?"
"I'm going to this meeting downtown in a few minutes, and I want you to go."
"What's it about, and how long will it last?"
"Oh, that's right, you have to work today, don't you?" she said "We should be done by noon, so you should have plenty of time to get ready and leave."
"Wait an minute, you didn't say where." I thought she was ready to hang up.
"Rita's café. Oh, by the way guess who's going to be there? Jim Mayberry, the husband of the dead wife/officer..."
"Why him, is this an official meeting?"
"Yes, it's a new organization to make better working conditions for women in the department of corrections. I would think you would be interested..."
"Listen, Di, I'm going to pass for now, if they heard about it we could be in trouble."
"All right, see you, but do you want to hear what is said from the meeting?"
"Well, yes, so why don't you call me and let me know tomorrow, or the next day."
Or never, I thought, I do not want to get myself killed.
"All right, see you, and be careful in there. Have a good day."
"Bye."

The leaves danced and skipped their way across the pavement as I drove to work. It was a warm fall day.
As I drove into the state parking lot, I noticed that the flag was at half-mast. A chill went up and down my spine. The last time I saw this was when officer Stoner was stabbed in the heart.
During briefing we were told that one of our veterans, Lt. Wainwright, of twenty years had committed suicide. Gossip had it that he was caught up into something. He couldn't find a way out, so he put a pistol to his head. The Captain didn't elaborate on what he was mixed up in, just that he took the fatal shot.
Yuk! There had to be another way, he was stupid, I thought. Almost a year had passed since I was hired, by now I had a good snitch. If I

gave him a treat from the machine up front, and he would tell me lots. He told me about an officer in his block that would take a prisoner in the catwalk; after the prisoner preformed oral sex, the officer would give him a twenty-dollar bill. He also told me that one of the teachers from the college was having sex with a prisoner while two of his 'homies' looked out for him.

"How do you know this, Jonsey?" I asked him.

"'Cause I be one of de look outs."

"I see."

I made it a point to get acquainted with the teacher he mentioned. She was professional in every way. She wore a wedding band. I had no reason to believe Jonsey, at least not right away.

Sometime later when I was working the bakery gate, during my rounds, the mess hall had been cleared, it was quiet, too quiet. The porters were mopping, one was singing, I could hear the mop slap on the floor, and the grating of the mop pail. Walking softly in that direction, lo, and behold, the dining room officer, Martha Brown, was in a clinch with a prisoner. They were so engrossed with their kissing that they didn't know I was there, thank God! Very quietly I crept back to my gate position and remained there until shift change. Officer Martha Brown was fired later for doing another stupid thing, nothing major, she was just stupid. My guess at the time was everyone has a weak moment. I couldn't help but think this was a bad example for any officer to do. This act could only be a detriment to the position of an officer, and weaken our control of the prisoners.

The teachers name was Sherry Plummer. She was slim, tall and had long wavy golden auburn hair. Sherry was a good friend of Deputy Warden Susan Lorenzo. After telling Sherry about the new organization, she expressed a desire to attend one of the meetings. I mentioned the organization Diane wanted me to join, Susan and Sherry both, wanted to attend one of the meetings. Susan was so interested in it she asked me out to lunch to discuss it.

We were to meet at a local oriental restaurant. I arrived just after Sue, who was already seated. Joining her, I opened the conversation.

"What's good to order, I've never been here before?" I asked.

"Oh," Susan laughed, "I usually order the chicken stir fry, it's really good."

"Okay, I'll try it," I replied, pondering over the menu.

"Tell me about this meeting. What do they call themselves?" Susan asked.

Right to the point, didn't even get a bite of food yet.

"Something about better working conditions for women in corrections. It came about after Officer Mayberry was killed, and an officer from the federal prison was raped. She was alone too," I answered.

"I would like to go with you, or meet you there, when you meet again with the group," Susan said.

"I'll bring this up to the officer in charge, so far it has just started up and I'm not sure what it really entails." I was evasive about quoting names just yet.

"I want you to trust me. I realize that you are hesitant to tell all. Yes, it is possible that this organization may conflict with the rules and regulations of our occupation. I shouldn't tell you this, but since you've been honest and open to discuss this with me, I'll go so far as to tell you something that is top secret. But I need your promise not to repeat anything I tell you."

"I think by now you know that I am the kind of person that can keep secrets. I am not called Father Flanagan for nothing. People confess to me often, I have never repeated anything I was told," I said.

She cleared her throat, hesitated for a second, and then said, "There are 12 FBI agents infiltrated in the prison right now investigating anything that might lead to…"

"What are they there for? Do the FEDS want to take over the state prisons?"

"Good question." Pause. "I'm not sure." *She knows, I shouldn't have interrupted, what are they looking for? Investigating what? Lead to what?*

"Are they officers, administration, or…?"

"You ask a lot of questions. Six prisoners, and six officers."

"Dangerous." I said feeling a flush rising to my face.

"Listen, I want to go to the next meeting with you, in the meanwhile if you see anything let me know, okay?"

"Sure." I replied.

"Our conversation is not to go beyond this place. No one is to know what was said today. No one. I want complete secrecy."

"Okay, sure. Promised."

We completed our meal and made small talk; the conversation did not go back to the opening discussion. An hour later we said good-bye.

Geez, did I do the right thing letting her know about this? Diane wanted me to talk around and put out feelers, see if anyone would be interested in joining. Well, she did tell me about the FBI men, I wonder how she knows about this? Is she one of them? Do DW's know everything?

Chapter 8

"Diane, it's Anne. What's happening? I haven't talked to you for at least two weeks."

"True. Guess what happened to me last week? I was called into Internal Investigations because of a note someone found. It was addressed to 'Blondie,' and out of five blonds, I was called on it. Ya, I was picked out of five blonds to be questioned."

"What did the note say?" I asked.

"It said, 'Thanks for the money. It came in handy, what with my mello being threatened and all.'"

"Oh, bull shit! You wouldn't do anything that stupid... you're just too intelligent to get mixed up in.."

"Ya, well, the truth is, I did, but I didn't tell I&I that," Diane said.

"Why? Why did you?"

"I believed him when he said his buddy was threatened and eminent death would result if he didn't pay his gambling debt."

"Dead over just twenty dollars, give me a break?" I said.

"Just last week prisoner Moton was killed just because he didn't pay back the three cigarettes he borrowed."

"I heard about it on the radio, but I don't know why he was killed. Did they catch the assailant?"

"No, there were too many prisoners, it was during chow lines. Shit, there was blood all over the place. Moton was struck in the juggler with a hand-made shank, and he just kept walking all the way from fourth gallery to the desk, where he fell dead on the spot. Bled to death that quick."

"So why did they call in the ambulance from downtown?"

"If he was pronounced dead, the body would have to lay there until Coroner Leighton was notified. It could take hours, you know there is only one coroner to cover a hundred mile radius. He lives exactly one hundred miles from the prison."

"I see, well that makes sense, but why did they put the paddles on him, that's what I heard?"

"It's true, just a pretense, until the ambulance from downtown arrived."

" Oh. That makes sense. Not to change the subject, but what I called for is I was wondering about that meeting you had last month. Are you going to have another one soon?" I asked.

"As a matter of fact we are meeting next Tuesday morning, ten o'clock at Rita's Café again."

"What did you talk about at the last meeting?"
"There were only three of us; the gal that was raped, Jim Mayberry, and me. Jim Mayberry had a lot to tell us about his wife's death."
"Oh, what was that?"
"She told him that she was being pressed for sex from a certain sergeant who said if she didn't get with the system she was on her own."
Thank God, I let that creep kiss me, I thought. *But I shouldn't have had to.... That's harassment.*
"What else, you said he told you a lot?"
"Well he said that there were three types of sperm in her body, but they were lost. Then there was a blond pubic hair found, although the alleged killer was black. No one heard anything, yet he believes there were people in the next room. Just a lot of funny cover-ups."
"Not that funny," I said.
"Strange."
"Yah, strange."
"And another thing, he said the radio that had all the blood on it wasn't the one that was issued to her that morning," She added.
"Now that's a bigee... someone really screwed up. The control center would know who had been issued that radio, wouldn't they?"
"Someone is protecting whom ever had that radio. We'll never know." Her voice trailed off.
" Did I tell you about the snitch telling me that officers killed her? Ya, I guess I did. This kind of confirms it. I don't like it. What the hell went on that she had to be killed?" I asked.
"Time might tell, and yet we may never know."
There was a moment of silence.
"Listen," I continued, "I want to tell you there are two women who are interested in coming to the next meeting; will this be alright?"
"Sure, who are they?"
"One is a teacher at the prison school, Sherry Plummer, and the other is DW Susan Lorenzo."
"No sh-t!"
"Right," I said.
"Well, anyone who is interested, is welcome, so let them come. They need to voice their needs too."
"You are right. And, they also work for the Department of Corrections, even if they are not officers."
"That's right." Diane answered.
"Okay, we'll see you Tuesday, if not sooner."

I had developed a great crush on one of the officers, who was constantly helping me. With Ralph wandering all over the country, I felt I needed male friendship at least. Don Black took me under his wing from the first day. I wasn't going to worry about whether I would be confronted with 'playing ball' with 'the system,' I wasn't going to hook-up with any of these creeps. Jonesy, my snitch, even was getting on my nerves, he hadn't told me that much. He hung around me more than I wanted him to. I didn't owe him anything. Now, his buddy who jogged a lot started talking to me. I really didn't want to be bothered. Besides I hadn't heard from Ralph, for over two years, so it was time I found someone.

Don and I talked often during slow times on the gun post. There was a phone at each unit. One night a group of hot air balloons flew in our direction. He called me on the phone and asked me if I saw them.
"If they get too close," he said, "We'll have to call the shift commander."
"Oh, that's right! They might attempt an escape, which would be a slow get away. Ha Ha!"
He echoed, 'ha,' "Course you heard about that helicopter that just pulled over the yard and away went the prisoner. Damn fool got caught thirty miles south of here in a bar, just a few hours later."
"They are always trying to escape, aren't they?" I asked.
"Yes, two years ago three escaped, some friend had a car waiting for them. There was a high-speed chase, which caused an accident. Two died instantly, the other one disappeared. About a year later a man held up a bank in Colorado, and guess who it was?"
"The third one?" I asked.
"That's right, the state was happy to hear that he was shot while attempting to rob the bank. Just proves the statistics that 81 percent of the criminals return to prison because of their habitual crimes," Don said.
"Well, tonight's payday." I changed the subject.
"Yes, what are you doing after work?" he asked.
"Probably go home, maybe stop for one beer with Jen." Diane sometimes met us too if we could get a connection.
"Listen, a group of us are going to Milo's later, why don't you come over there?" Don asked.
Wow! This was it! What I wanted him to ask for some time now.
"I'll see if Genevive wants to, we'll talk about it."
"Well, she doesn't need to be there, if she hesitates."

"Oh, we always stop on payday, even if it is just for a hamburger and a cola."
"Okay. I'll save you both a seat," Don said.
"Alright." I couldn't help smiling to myself.

"Milo's is out of our way," Genevive said with a pout.
"Yes, but he's saving a seat, he expects 'us' to be there."
"Okay, just this once. He really must be something. I'll follow you, I don't know the way." She replied.
The day was over. We punched out, and went to Milo's.
Even though the place was jammed, it was easy to find Don, with his white wavy hair, and those dark brown eyes.
"Genevieve, this is Don, he works the gun posts all the time." I pointed to Genevive and said, "And Genevive works in P.C." (Protective Custody)
"I see, how do you do Genevive? Can I order you something?"
"Yes, we'll have Miller Lite," I said.
While he was ordering Genevive said, " This is why you are here?" Pointing her thumb at Don.
"Yes, I like him."

41

Chapter 9

Jim Mayberry answered his door.
"Hello, my name is Max Idleman, I work for the State Insurance Company, and may I come in?"
"Er, I guess so," he let him through. "Here have a seat." Don gestured towards the kitchen table on the other side of the living room.
Pulling out two chairs, they both sat down.
Mayberry poured two cups of coffee, after asking him if he would like some. He knew that there was a lot of money coming his way, 250,000 to be exact. He knew he should keep on the right side of this guy.
"Well, Mr. Mayberry I have a few questions to ask you," Max Idleman said.
"Like what?"
"Well, as you know, you are beneficiary for the insurance in the amount of 250,000 dollars as a result of your wife's death. Providing, that she was killed in the line of duty. My job is to prove or dis- prove the liability of the state."
"Well, she sure as hell was killed in there! How could you possibly question the fact?"
"Isn't it a fact that you were married before, Mr. Mayberry?"
"Yes, but what does that have to do with it?"
"Isn't it a fact that your first wife had a lot of money?"
"Yes, but..."
"And, isn't it a fact that she is dead also?"
"Of natural causes, what are you trying to infer?"
"Nothing at all, Mr. Mayberry, but the question of the inheritance has come up."
"You've really done your homework haven't you Mr. Idleman?"
"What I understand is that you have a child. A girl from your first marriage, and since she is a minor, you would be power of attorney over the inheritance until she is of age. Or out of college."
"So what...what does this have to do with my recent wife's death and the insurance involved?"
"Er, ah, just a minute Mr. Mayberry, ah. Are you aware that the will was changed since you divorced your first wife, and before she died?"
"I don't know anything about it, and I think it's time you left."
"One last question, did you have anything to do with your wife's murder?"
"Get out! Get out, I'll sue you for slander!"

Mr. Idleman was on his feet, out the door and half way off the porch, with papers all askew poking out of his briefcase. His tie was flying in mid-air, with a half frenzied look in his eyes.

What are you doing, Jim Mayberry thought, I'll never get the money unless I ....

"Wait, wait, come back here." Jim said.

Idleman stopped and turned with a surprised look.

"Will you answer my questions?" Idleman asked.

"First, Mr. Idleman, I want you to believe me when I say I don't know anything about, err, referring to my first marriage, the will."

"Alright, you don't. You are not aware that if the old man dies before your daughter Michelle is of age, you are the sole heir of the entire estate, business and any investment income right up until his death? Of course your daughter will be the sole benefactor at your death."

"Ah, not for sure, so what is the change?" Jim acted ignorant of the true facts.

Here it comes. I know, but it may incriminate me if I admit it.

"A clause stating that you must not be married at the time that he expires."

"Preposterous! Michelle should have it coming to her without any reason."

I have to convince him, Lord help me, Jim thought.

"And, I might also add that the sum the state will give you is enough in itself to... er..."

He's right, Jim thought. *Keep trying; Jim, or you're going to lose it. He is an ass hole, and a thorough one at that.*

"Do you have any idea how much I loved my wife? I left all that prestige and money for her. She was the joy of my life. I miss her so much you'll never know; my whole life was built around her. Now all I have is my daughter, Michelle."

"Why did a witness say that your marriage was on the rocks? You aren't a spring chicken, you know, she was young enough to be your very young daughter."

"Gossip. Gossip, I swear we were happy," Jim ranted.

"Isn't it true that she was supporting you?" asked Idleman.

"I was working, it didn't pay much, but I was working," Jim said.

"One day a week?"

"Listen, why does whether I work or not have to do with the insurance money?"

"Maybe something, I'll talk it over with my associates. You will hear from the company office, after I turn in my report."

43

"But wait, are you aware that I've been threatened, my home shot at, my truck windshield smashed in…" Mayberry went on.

"Can you prove any of this?"

Jim hung his head, "No. This makes me worry for my daughter. My concern for her safety is another issue. I just wish this was all over with."

"Well, I'm sorry Mr. Mayberry, but I can only use the facts."

Jim was still looking at the floor when Mr. Idleman left.

Chapter 10

Fall had arrived. It was a cloudy day that almost looked like it could snow, but it was too early for that. It was Thursday and I was assigned to the checkpoint gate between the cell blocks and yard.
I arrived at my gate and I talked a few minutes to the day Officer. He said the day had gone without incident; everything was routine.
"Have a good one, " he called over his shoulder as he rounded the building to go to his truck, and home.
There was a straggler passing through with a pass to the gymnasium, which was adjacent to the Chow Hall. The prisoners went there to exercise, play basketball, cards and other things. They usually stayed there until the chow lines began around five o'clock.
Industries would break out next and I would open the gate for them, as was the usual way of doing when mass movement was in process. The prison workers had already been through a checkpoint, frisked for contraband, and sent on their way to the Block, where they would wait for chow.
Closing the gate, I saw the yard crew coming my way. The Sergeant called to me and said that after yard and lockdown at nine p.m., I would need to go to Industries with three other officers to shake down the area.
I said, "Okay, Sarg."
Chow lines began about 15 minutes later, my radio buzzed.
"15, I'm sending 'C' Block for chow."
"Copy," I said. I opened the gate and stood back to let half a block of prisoners at a time pass, approximately 250 prisoners. This continued until the next half went by. The Dining Room Sergeant called to see if the lines had gone past, if so he would send the first half of 'D' Block and so on until the entire Prison was fed and back in the cells.
Yard started at 7:30 p.m. and once again the gate would be opened wide until they were passed through, then I would lock it and wait. Stragglers from the dining room workers would go through, checking them for their pass and any food that inmate workers may have taken from the chow hall.
One time the worker obviously had something between his legs, the bulge was greater that normal! I asked him for a shake down, he squirmed and really didn't want to.
"Not there, officer, that's my private area."
"Well, if you don't have anything there prove it."

He pulled out approximately eight pieces of fried chicken, wrapped in tin foil. I took the chicken and threw it in the trash barrel.
"Aw, now you ruined perfectly good yard bird, " he said. Wandering towards his cellblock, he looked back and gave me a disdainful glance.
It wasn't more that two minutes later after the dining room worker reached the block that my phone rang. It was Officer Owens, from 'C' Block.
"Why did you take my chicken and throw it in the trash?"
"Hey, if you really want it, and will eat it after it was in a prisoner's crotch, just come and get it from the trash barrel,"
"I never thought of it that way." He said.
"I'm sorry, officer Owens, I didn't know it was for you."
"It's alright" I could hear the disappointment in his voice as he said it, he probably was hungry.
"Yup," I said.
I'll never forget it! I grinned.

Time had lapsed from that day. It was fall again. I was at the checkpoint gate.
It turned dark during chow lines, and was getting cooler. Fall truly had set in. I sat in my shack to warm up, a half hour had passed. There hadn't been any traffic since the prisoners went to yard. I poked my head out to see if anyone was around the corner, when I realized it was quiet. Usually I could hear the prisoners playing basketball, shouting across to each other, the yard crew routinely kept busy stopping tattoo action in the corner of the back fence, watching for predators, anything else that would warrant a ticket, or a need to deter anything that may be stirring up amongst them.
Tonight it was quiet.
Dead still!
Usually the control center would call half time on the loud speakers that were placed on each corner of the roofs of the buildings, and then if any of the prisoners wanted to go back to their cell they could.
No half time.
Strange. I thought.
I knew all the yard crew was on the yard, about then I noticed one officer coming from the chapel, walking slowly, and looking in the direction of the yard, he looked at me and motioned for me to meet him.
He reached me before I was to the corner of the building, and said,
 "Have you seen what's going on out there?"

"I noticed that it was quiet, but, and they haven't called half time."
"Ya, the damn prisoners have the yard crew in the center of the yard. They are surrounded by the Moors, and all the prisoners have formed a big circle around the outside up against the fence."
We both looked in that direction.
He added, "The Moors are in the center guarding the officers. I can't hear what they are saying…"
 Sergeant Small, the yard sergeant, was a married man with a family, his wife was pregnant for their fourth child, he was hoping for a boy this time. Officer Bruno was a tall quiet man. I knew he was married but he didn't say a lot about it. He had a compassionate aura. Once I saw him give the yardman a lunch cake, he looked at me, grinned and said, " It doesn't hurt to have a comrade in here…"
Officer Sam Dwyer was a wiry fellow in his late 40's, who found a shank if it was anywhere around him, he drew to them like a magnet, he was 'the best' in my opinion. Officer Porter was young but brave; he had blond curly hair, light blue eyes, even though he seemed to be shy, he did a great job. I worried about all of them during this time they were surrounded by the near one thousand obviously upset prisoners. The prisoners were stirring up momentum.

The Moors were one of three Gangs in the prison. Milanics, and Nuestra Familia were the other two of the three major gangs. The Moors held the power over the three gangs. They controlled any and all authority among the prisoners.

About then we heard,
"All for one and one for all!"
"UNITY, UNITY, UNITY!"
 They kept repeating it, over and over. Shivers crept over my back. I could hear words from the 'Holy Koran' I guessed, although I didn't recognize them. The goose bumps weren't from the chill in the air, although there was a chill and the fall dew was setting in.
"Them sons-o-bitches, they better not harm the crew," officer Winthers said.
 He was a tall man in his forties, and 'a cop before he came in here,' is what he told me.
By now, we both were at a vantage point where we could see part of what was going on. The Moors would get their heads together and talk, then go out individually to different sections of the prisoners, then in unison they would commence to shout again.
"United we stand, divided we fall".

Louder and louder the shouting vibrated against the buildings and re-vibrated back.

"What do they want? What?"

"I don't know, but I'm sure we will know before long, I'm going in there."

Holy cow, what is happening, and what is going to happen? The adrenalin began to flow.

Now it was past nine o'clock, long past time for total lock down, final count to clear in the block before shift change.

No one moved, they just stood there. Dead silence then the prisoners shouted more. I found myself pacing back and forth, realizing it wouldn't help. The next thing I know I was pacing again.

Why? What? There should be more than four officers to control this many prisoners.

I thought it would never end.

I could feel a sickness in my stomach.

I pushed back the cuff of my jacket and blazer, to see what time it was.

Nine twenty.

Finally at almost nine thirty, the Captain's voice boomed over the loud speakers, "Yard is now over, all prisoners return to the block!"

At first there was no response. Finally, the entire one thousand prisoners began to leave the yard.

My heart jumped, they started to leave, advancing toward the gate at the corner of the yard.

I had to open the checkpoint gate to let them through.

Leaving Withers at the corner of the building, I quickly returned the twenty feet to the checkpoint gate and opened it.

It was still quiet.

I didn't know they were leaving the yard until I saw the entire group, marching in formation towards me, led by the Moors

The Moors led them!

None of them were talking, all wore a solemn look, and my heart rushed to my throat.

Here they are all marching at me and I realized that I am completely alone.

Alone!

The yard crew was nowhere to be seen, no one has called me on the phone, nor radioed me, nothing. The men on the roof must be there; although it was so dark it was impossible to see anyone.

Dear Lord, protect me.

It would only take one, just one to take me hostage, oh dear God, I'm scared I thought. Would the turret guards shoot if they grabbed me? Would they miss and shoot me instead?
They could take me hostage, kill me, brutalize and mutilate me. All this anxiety for a measly $32,000 a yea job, what am I doing here?
My hands shook uncontrollably, my heart jumped into my throat. I felt like I was choking. I couldn't get my breath, my body shook, I was trembling and saying, keep calm, smile at them, something. Lord, I better get in the shack.
Ha! They could knock it over without effort. There was no lock on it. Besides this would look like you are scared, thoughts continued to fly through my mind. It seemed like it was taking forever for them to get up to me if I smile this wouldn't work. Just stand there with no expression.

So I just stood there. It seemed like it took forever for them to, just one nut could change everything. I could be rushed, and subdued very easily with that many criminals, rapists, murders, thief's, child molesters, scum of the earth! Finally they all passed.

I quickly shut and locked the gate, secured the area, and logged all events of this evening in the logbook.

They're gone. I thought.

No one would know what I felt at that moment when they were at my gate. Approximately six abreast, the prisoners were marching straight past me to their blocks.

The yard crew made their way out.

The Sergeant was smiling at me; everything was okay according to him.

"Sarg, what was this all about?"

"They were demonstrating because they were cold and the construction wasn't finished, windows out, poor boys."

The prison officials planned to replace the unsafe old windows. The cold weather set in and it was not complete.

"Well, they .."

"You did a good job," Sergeant Small said, "As soon as we come back from the blocks, sign out and meet us in the control center."

"Okay."

My heart was still a few inches above its normal position.

I was alone! Damn it!

I arrived at the control center; the Captain told us that the Governor was called, when this all began. The Governor gave permission to put

two gun squads on the roof above me, watching, in case something happened.
Why didn't they call me? I had a phone and no one, no one called me.
We were excused. I punched out, headed for my car and drove home. I was numb.
I drove in a stupor; I was half way home when I finally realized it. The chest pains had finally subsided, I could breathe easily again.
I'm okay, nothing happened, it's all right, nothing happened, and I'm safe.
The tears flowed down my cheeks and sobs kept coming for some time.

Finally the sobs diminished. I had a lot to think about.
Think positive thoughts, always positive. The bright side of this event is that I didn't have the tedious job of shaking down industries for once. I smiled to myself. *And another day at the 'Cest Pool' was over.* I heaved a sigh of relief.

"Mean Joe Brown has come to town'", the prisoners chanted after the state representative had departed and returned to the capitol.
We were instructed at roll call the next day that Representative Joe Brown had arrived at the prison with orders to take a tour. Lieutenant Parker was in charge of the control center, while Captain Bartholomew escorted Representative Joseph Brown on a general tour of the prison. By 2 p.m. a decision was made and related to the afternoon shift: yard time would be divided into five separate locations with fences separating the bulk of the population.
Receiving and Guidance Center, Protective Custody, B-C-D-and E Block would each have their allotted time at intervals.
This was the conclusion for a deterrent to prevent any future demonstrations.

Chapter 11

Industries are the part of the prison where all the furniture is made for all state offices. Including the Social Services, Secretary of State and Department of Corrections. Other items manufactured there are state shoes, made for officers and prisoners, and license plates.
This gave reason to have a two-gated 'Shake Down Shack', a 12-foot fence with wire on top, similar to barbed wire with razor sharp edges, to prevent escape.
The gates had metal detectors. The prisoners were instructed to empty their pockets. If the detector went off, the prisoner would be shook down physically. This seemed to bring the shank material down to 3% at least. Somehow we still found shanks in the housing areas.
 One day at roll call, Captain Wiggins told about young prisoner Martin, who was sent to Jamestown because he was a repeat offender. He honestly looked like a 14 year old; blue eyes, blond hair, and a look of innocence. His first crime was B & E. He was sent to a camp, but ran away, so he was put in a prison with young offenders. When he saw the chance, he ran away again. Now he was here with hardcore prisoners. Recently he was caught building a cardboard fort in the industries area. He stayed there for twenty-four hours, until he was found. I guess you could say he took a sabbatical, or a hunger strike, but there was no way out from there.

The Jamestown Centenal wrote an article on the escape. 'Two guards suspended after escape' Oct 7, 1989.
It went on to say that the guards were suspended for one week without pay, they weren't suspended for assisting the a prisoner escape, it was because the Sgt. was responsible for making sure the prisoner had returned to their cell, and the other officer was suspended because he gave inaccurate information about the sergeants involvement in the escape. The spokesperson for prison affairs stated that when the officers were cleared of wrongdoing, they would receive the pay withheld."
As far as I can remember the one prisoner showed up within a few hours, while Martin stayed in industries for 24 hours until he was caught.

Near industries was the loading dock. I was assigned there only once when working overtime, which usually started at eight o'clock and finished at 4 p.m. Trucks brought in supplies, materials for industries and food and supplies for the mess hall kitchen and the like.

One of the female officers that came in after my group worked this shift everyday. She was small, like me, but carried the job well.

One afternoon I was working on a gun post on the wall, directly above the dock where trucks unloaded pipes, etc. to repair the steam heating system. I noticed the little female officer Carter was driving the big truck, backing it down the ramp into the lower level. The next thing I hear on the radio, was a code 10 in back loading dock. From my angle I couldn't see what was happening. The nose of the truck stuck out, but that was the only visible part of it. Officer McKay came running from the other side of the wall, to see what was happening.

"Did you hear?" he asked.

"What?" I replied.

"Officer Carter was backing down the ramp to the lower level, when the brakes failed to work, the steel went through the cab and through her. The truck descended down to the cement dock causing the steel pipes to jam against it. One pipe was three feet longer than the rest. When it hit the cement wall it drove it straight back through the cab. The ambulance is on its' way. They will have to wait until then to cut the pipe off and take her downtown.

" Can't see much here can you, I'd better get back to my Post," he was already ambling back to his post, shaking his head back and forth, "It was a freak accident."

"Right." I agreed, " I'll hang here until time for chow lines."

I prayed for her.

Fortunately there was very little prisoner movement. My concentration was focused on her and my talk with God.

Soon the ambulance arrived, Carter was loaded and taken to the hospital downtown. She underwent extensive surgery, and was in the hospital for recovery and rehabilitation, for two months.

Later I heard that she was on disability and would not return to work.

I set my alarm clock, so I could rise early, do my chores around the house, go to the Better Working Conditions For Women in Corrections meeting and still be ready for work on time. I would only get six hours of sleep, but it would give me time to do chores I had been putting off. Finally I was cleaned up and ready to attend the

Better Working Conditions For Women in Corrections meeting, which Diane had told me about. It was exactly 5 minutes before 10 o'clock when I arrived at Rita's Café.
I did tell both ladies, Sherry and Susan, about the meeting and said I planned to attend. I wasn't sure what this so-called group planned to do to make things better. I was sure of one thing, though, there would be a lot of input from everyone. I sat with my back to the wall, a custom I inherited by the time I had worked 2 years 'inside.' This was also a vantage point, I could see anyone who entered. The cafe expected Diane to be there already. Diane walked through the door with a man I believed to be Don Mayberry.
"Hi, Diane, good to se you."
"Hi, this is Don Mayberry, you know…"
"Yes, how do you do?"
"As well as could be expected, I guess." he said.
Am I detecting a downer? Let's be positive, boy.
"Are Sherry & Susan coming?" Diane asked.
"They said they would, the traffic could have held them up." I answered.
"Don was just telling me that he was having a tough time getting his insurance check from the company."
"Really! It's been over two years hasn't it?" I asked.
"The insurance man, Idleman, fears being bilked out of the money like it was his own, " Don said.
"Well, is that unusual, or does this happen often?"
"Who knows," he said. "One thing for sure is there aren't that many claims. Only two in the last two years."
Two more women walked in the door. Diane stood up and went to greet them, pulling out chairs and introducing her.
"Anne, I want you to meet Sybil Drake, she is the one who started this organization, and this is Yvonne, who wants to join today. This is Anne Morgan from Jamestown." Diane motioned at me.
I nodded at them both and said, "How do you do?"
Diane continued by introducing the two women to Don also. Sybil remained standing.
"Lets order coffee and wait to see if anyone else comes," Sybil said.
Sybil took over; she was that sort of person. She wore a dominating demeanor.
It probably made that rapist feel good to have control over this very assertive person. I heard that her rapist was an officer. Was she like many other women, who put on a good front? According to Diane she

53

was extremely intelligent. She had all the plans to organize at the first meeting.

Our coffee was served, we fixed it to taste, and made small talk until everyone was there. At 10:15, three more women walked in, giggling as they passed through the door.

It was Sherry, Susan, and I recognized the librarian in the prison school.

"Hi, girls, over here, who's the extra?" I asked.

"This is Vivian Green, she is the librarian at the prison school." Susan glanced around to all of us and continued, "And I am DW Lorenzo, this lady to my right is Sherry Plummer, who also works at the school, as a teacher."

We exchanged greetings.

Sybil started reading the notes from the past two meetings; there were only three present for those. She said many were skeptical about joining because of the repercussions that could affect them at their work place. This was precisely the purpose of the organization, to make repercussions stop.

"To stop sexual harassment, stop being assigned in locations that were dangerous to women as well as men," she said.

"Wait a minute, we knew it would be dangerous when we were hired," I interrupted.

Diane interjected, "Yes, we knew, but how many times so far have you been in a situation that you didn't feel comfortable in?"

"Several," I said.

"That's what I mean."

"Well, so far it has worked out okay," I said.

Don stood up and said, "My wife is dead. She was alone when it happened. She was told to play ball. She told me that the night before she was murdered. Many of the officers were pressing her for sexual favors. The day she was killed, she was sent to an assignment that she had never been on before, with no clue what it entailed. She was handed a radio, and told to keep the prisoners in custody. If you don't see why we want to organize, to try to correct these mistakes, then don't join. But please hear Sybil, and Diane out."

Mayberry's forehead was furrowed into a frown. It was the most he said about his wife since it had happened.

"What does it entail, to join?" Susan asked.

"Just fill out the application, and hand it in at the next meeting. Bring a guest, talk to others, and let's see who may be interested in what we are doing," Sybil said.

"Each of us has had something happen 'in there' that was not expected, nor warranted. Think about it. You can't keep quiet, or it will continue just as it is," Diane said.

My head was looking like a windshield wiper back and forth from Don, to Diane, to Sybil, and back to Don again.

We all had had some kind of experience that should not be swept under the carpet and forgotten. There is a thin line between what is or is not dangerous, or sexual harassment, or both.

We broke into small conversations. Susan leaned over and said, "I need to talk to you, can you stay a little longer?"

"Yes, as you can see, I'm ready to leave for work from here."

I could hear Don talking about the insurance company giving him a scare. He was sure he wouldn't get the check.

Diane was talking about the time she was approached for sexual favors. The male officer made her feel threatened. He justified it, because he was wearing a pistol when he approached her. As a result of the attack, she took it to court. Many at court were smirking and found it amusing. He was found not guilty.

Sybil handed out applications when the meeting ended.

When the group left, we stood saying our good-byes and Susan turned to me and said, "Let's order lunch, we can sit closer to the kitchen to eat."

"Did Sherry and Yvonne ride with you?" I asked.

"No, they rode together."

"Great, that will leave us to talk freely about what you mentioned."

We ordered and waited for lunch. Don, and Diane left. It was just Susan and I.

"What did you want to talk about?" I asked.

"One of the officers, a female, backed out of 'the 12', I'm wondering if you will take her place?"

"Did he say why? What makes you think I can do it?"

"She was afraid of being caught. She didn't believe she had the 'guts' to face what may arise."

"She? I don't blame her. And again, what makes you think I can do it?"

"It isn't hard, just do what I tell you to."

"Like what?"

"First watch a certain officer. She has brought attention to herself, and to me. I want to know what she does, where she goes, whom she talks to. That's enough for now. I will tell you in time why I need this information."

"So you want me to be a snitch."
"Nooooooo! Not a snitch. It is very important that I know what's going on. There is more here than you realize." She said.
"I'll do what I can. Who do I have to watch?"
"Officer Julia Brown. Do you know her?" Susan asked.
"Briefly, she works in housing, I'm in custody, so I don't see her often." I said, nodding my head.
"Keep your eyes open."
In later years, I realized that you should never volunteer anything, and give the least amount of information as possible. I was young and naive, and this was one good way to get noticed. An officer who would take pride in doing the very best I possibly could. I respected Susan because she was intelligent and had reached a very high level of responsibility and authority.
Driving to work later gave me time to mentally replay what happened at the meeting.
I got from Don that he was more concerned about getting the insurance check. Diane, God bless her, was upset because they laughed at her about the sexual harassment case.
Susan was more interested in catching a female officer doing something she wasn't ready to disclose to me yet?
Sybil, I believe, wants to get back at everyone who has taken her pride away, and will take down anyone who is willing to join up and stick his or her neck out for her cause. She is disgruntled about the working conditions, but I need to get into focus, and realize this is a very different job and environment. If I join, would I be a pawn to her gain. Am I the sucker with my neck out? Ugh!
I read Sybil's notes. She shared her experience with us in a written document. Diane gave me a copy of them. She wrote write the notes each night. She worked the midnight shift and wrote in a journal after her shift. Her notes indicated that her worst enemy was not the residents, but her co-workers.
'When she went on shift the residents were in lock down. Most were sleeping. There was a head count around 3 a.m., and nothing again until wake-up at shift change. Her co-workers on the other hand were men, and what do men think of every thirty seconds? Since Sybil was young, good looking, and built well, she was fair game. She worried about which one she would write up for sexual harassment first. This was her basis for the new organization.

Chapter 12

I asked myself why I should join the forces? Why should I be one of the twelve? It wouldn't pay more. However there would be some satisfaction in doing what was right.
It would mean I would be watching every single one of my co-workers. It would also mean that I could be in danger, at any given time. Even though that was already the case.
Of course there are a few things. First, I had already said I wanted to be the very best officer, do what was right, and always keep the rules of the game honest.
Second, there is the incident at the bar one night. I had had two Pepsi Colas, told some good jokes, and made everyone laugh. The group was getting drunk, so I said my excuses and left. The next day at work I was accused of messing with my best friends car, at least I thought of her as my best friend. Other cars were messed up, one had tires flattened, another was scratched with a key, also that night. Mine would have been too, had I not gone home early. Genevive thought it was I who did the dirty deed. I was disappointed in her and everyone else who believed I was the culprit. I wasn't bitter, just disappointed.
In time she buried the hatchet. I never was a bar hopper, nor a drinker, so I don't miss going.

Third, Don said I was too good for him, and started dating a fat gal who worked in accounting, up front. They were good for each other; they both liked the bar scene, and she could give him the gossip from the front offices. I didn't find out about Don and 'Miss Piggy' until the Christmas party, three months later.
Another situation that distanced me from my co-workers happened one evening after work. I purchased a new automobile, and didn't want to put miles on it, so I paid to car pool with four guys, who lived in a town further up the road. I waited in the car with the driver for the other three. He told me that they had all voted, and didn't want me to ride with them anymore, because it took an extra 10 minutes and gas. I said I would pay more, but the vote was in. I took it like a man; at least they thought I did. That wasn't so bad. A short time later, the entire shift was lined up to go out the gate, approximately 280 of the crew, one officer I knew briefly, and never worked with, turned to me and said,
"What do you think you are, a man?"

"What?" I asked.

"You want to ride with the guys, act like a guy; they need their time alone without a woman hanging around, Morgan," he yelled at me.

Everyone heard. I just shook my head like I didn't know what he was talking about. I knew, the guys needed their space and it probably was an inconvenience to come a quarter mile off the main highway to pick me up.

I was angry. Not just angry with the officer who shouted those words at me, but at the four that told him. What was the point?

After that night I realized everyone was not like me, and that it takes several types of people to want to work in a place like that.

One of the guys I used to ride with was later fired for bringing in dope. One stopped riding with them to share rides with me. He later was killed at the wheel when he fell asleep one night. Fortunately for me it was my night off.

Most of the officers were good people that I could trust to back me up in a clinch. But the bad seed can pull you down to their level if you allow it.

I still wanted to go down as one of the best officers, doing what I was told. There were a small number of officers who made it rough for me and other female co-workers. I felt lucky that I didn't have to work with them that often. I had great partners most of the time.

The captain frequently asked me to do special assignments. A break from the 'front lines' made my job more pleasant.

After weighing everything on my list of experiences, I decided I wouldn't be hurting anyone if I took the assignment with the Deputy Warden. If the officers and administration were clean, they had nothing to worry about, if they were dirty shame on them. If my reports lead to their arrest, they probably would never know it was from what I saw and reported. Most of all, I realized it didn't matter what others thought, how I felt, or what I did.

As long as I was satisfied with myself, and had a clear conscience, it would work. I decided to talk to Susan as soon as possible. I already knew who to watch and what she needed.

I had seen enough blood and guts to last me a lifetime.

The prisoners could be entertaining.

One would stand on his bunk and 'cat call' that he would 'do it' for a Little-Debbie.

Another was in love with one of the nurses and when she didn't give him the time-of-day, he cut his penis off and ate it. When asked why, he said that he believed it would grow out bigger. An ex-ray proved he really did swallow it.
There were the hackers, always slitting their wrists, and others shoving shanks into their enemies. I was tired of it. A new assignment would be refreshing; it could take my mind off the worst and give new insight to my endeavors.

The next assignment Tuesday was in the gun turret above 'D' block. It fit into the middle of the ceiling of the fourth Gallery, literally hanging 50 feet in the air.
Steps descended down into the "submarine" that hung above the block. It was a great vantage point. I could see most parts of the block, with very little exception.
As I signed the logbook, I looked back a few days to see what entries were jotted down, checking to for any incidents I was not aware of.
It was quiet when I arrived; just before chow hall workers were released to prepare dinner. Residents would be returning from industries, library, craft shop, gymnasium, chapel, or afternoon yard, keeping me busy until they were locked in. Soon it was five o'clock; time for chow. Some of the prisoners were 'on top lock,' which was a form of loss of privileges. Top lock was when an officer gallery would manually lock the upper lock of an individual cell. The prisoner would not be able to go out when the entire gallery was released automatically from the end of the gallery.
I could hear the metallic sound of a slam against the metal wall and each officer would yell,
"Fourth"
The prisoners would know that the lock was off and they could leave for the chow hall.
For a few seconds it was a free for all. Some didn't intend to go to chow, but went out of their cell anyway, to talk to their 'homie,' and quickly returned before an officer walked down and slammed their door shut.
Most of the prisoners went to chow, only a few remained.
I looked out from one peek hole to another, checking, and noticing each exchange, making sure all went well. The officers would go to third gallery. Slamming the crank on the end of the gallery, and yell,
"Third."
This continued until the entire block had been released for dinner.

I watched officers, Henry, Marks and Robinson put their coat on and leaves the block for dinner break. Two minutes later Officer Robinson returned to the block, took his coat off and hung it up near the Sergeants desk. I relaxed and sat down for a few minutes, since it wouldn't be very long before their return.

Jingle. Jingle. What? It was the noise of keys as the officer ascended the stairs. I looked out and saw Officer Robinson, the arrogant one, walking up from the desk to third gallery. He had a cocky way of walking, a swagerish swing to discribe it. Suddenly he stopped, unlocked a cell, and went in for about two minutes.

I supposed he was shaking the cell down for contraband, doing a routine check. When he came out he had a can of soda. He swaggered up closer and unlocked another cell, went in. Was he doing another shake down? No, he came out with a bag of chips. Two cells farther he stopped and talked to a prisoner, in about three minutes he reached into the cell and came out with a sandwich. He also had confiscated a newspaper. He smiled to himself as he wandered on down to the opposite end of the bulkhead and sat at a desk. There he ate and read the news.

What was wrong with this? I asked myself. The soda pop and chips were stolen, obviously, because the resident was not in his cell. Buying food from a prisoner was chancy, it could be tainted, with no refrigeration, it could have been spoiled.

This was against the rules of our job; he was looking at possible discipline. Some 'homie' would certainly miss his paper, however he could return it before chow lines were back.

Most of all it was against the rules! Next I watched him take something from the newspaper, a package, and put it in his shirt. I could do one of three things; tell the Sergeant, tell my snitch in 'D' block, or third, not tell anyone anything.

I brought my lunch when I worked in a gun turret; I nibbled on pickled beets and tuna fish from a plastic dish, drank water from my thermos, and crunched on raw carrots.

Chow lines were in; and soon it was time for yard.
"9 to 14," I recognized the yard sergeant's voice calling my radio number.
"14,"
"I'm sending yard your way."

"Copy." I responded, glancing at my watch. It was 6:30. I stepped out of my shack to the edge of the roof where I had a closer advantage point, for traffic control. It was a routine day without incident.
Yard came in at 8:30 and total lock down for count at 9:00. The rest of the shift passed quickly. After the prisoners were off the yard there was very little to do; jotting a few notes in the log, cleared out, and moved up to the top gun post which overlooked the entire prison and was at least two stories higher than the roof level. We, the officers from each post, stayed there until it was time to descend to the main front gate, then control center, where we would punch out.

It was a quiet day at work. It was payday and everyone was restless to get through the gate and on his or her way.
"Come on, come on. What's the holdup?" I heard one of the officer's shout. I stood inside the gate with about 15 other officers and Shift Commander Jones.
"Okay, you six," pointing at me and Pluff, Daniels, Alve, Cortez and McTaggart, "into the arsenal, were doing six strip searches."
"What else on payday night?" I heard an officer complain, as we were ushered in.
"Okay, girls," Captain Jones said, "if you co-operate this shouldn't take long. Take everything out of your pockets, take off your shoes and clothes."
We were all females. I took off my clothes while a bogus officer from front desk had her hands all over me, everywhere including my cracks. I immediately felt hatred for her. Indignation crept over me. *How did this look, not only to all six girls, but also to the other officers who saw us being ushered into the arsenal? I knew assumptions would buzz around the prison like wild fire.*
We were told later that it was to absolve any harassment complaints.
Bull shit! One of the six was suspicious, or this wouldn't have happened. Harassment, maybe, if they only pulled out the one that was suspected. Yes, I could see that.
I went home and watched TV for a while, to gear down before going to bed.

The next day the whole prison was buzzing with what happened. Some of it the truth and most of it rumor.
"Hello, Anne, dis be Della. You be hearin' any of da gossip?" I called her DD for short.
"Not really." I lied, wanting to hear what she had heard.
"Well you know sister Pluff, who is from my town, they say she be all wrapped up in dope smugglin'.' Dey find a note on her that say 'thank

you, there will be a car outside waitin' to give you your money.' She swear she didn't do it, but it look bad, you hear what I sayin'?"

"They won't fire her unless they find more than that, doesn't seem…"

"They already offer her to resign!"

"No kidding, did she?"

"Well, she be thinkin' 'bout it. Cause you see she will be hit by every bro in here, now to bring in somethin' or other."

"Probably so, oh, that is a dirty shame. It reflects on all us females. So many things have happened since we came in here. Look at that Sgt. from day shift, she was set up big time, and now she's history."

"We got to be careful, dese prisoners pick on us, 'cause we be wimmin, and de male o'cers won back us up. Di's not an easy place to work, Anne."

"I know. It's like keep your eyes and ears open, your back covered and your mouth shut."

"Don' dat be da truth." Della's voice trailed.

I loved her accent.

I liked Della, she was always truthful, loyal, and told me everything.

Chapter 13

I missed the next meeting for Better Working Conditions for Women in Corrections. There were just too many things for me to do, in my two days off. I really wanted to go because of all that is happening.
 My little snitch was transferred out, but his buddy, Jerry, was talking to me more he would tell me how the dope was brought in.
When Officer Robinson from helped himself to prisoners' things in the cells while they were at chow, or at yard. Some of the prisoners told the Sergeant about it; not all the prisoners went to chow. Officer Robinson was called in about it, and his response was that I was the one who told on him. "The officer in the turret,' was what he said. Sergeant Johnson called me immediately and asked if I saw him go into any cells. I said that I thought that he was doing routine shake downs, but found it unusual for him to come out with food.
Officer Robinson approached me in the control center later.
"You will be sorry for telling," he said in a low voice.
Jonesy, my snitch, heard him say that to me. He was always hanging around pretending that he was policing the area, carrying a black trash bag in his hip pocket. This time he was hanging at the snack machine right out the hall from the C.C.
"You watch, he be in big trouble if he try anythin' again." said Jonesy.
"You watch da next time you work the turret, Officer Morgan."
"I didn't hear that," I politely said.
Sure enough, the next time I worked the turret, Officer Robinson took a sandwich from a cell. He ate it before going back to the Sergeant's desk. He looked like he was staggering instead of swaggering though as he started down the next flight of steps he fell, tumbling the last eight or nine steps. He was unconscious. I called to the desk officer and two officers ran to him. An ambulance arrived and rushed and him down town to pumped his stomach.

The next day's scuttle but was that he had marijuana, and morphine in his blood. They could have killed him, but he lived. I never had trouble from him again, and, he didn't have that cocky attitude anymore.
That was the last 'favor' Jonsey did for me before he was transferred. Jerry, Jonsey's friend, claimed that a female officer had brought in 6,000 dollars worth of cocaine.

"You know Jerry, I just don't know how she brought it in to the tune of six... , if in fact she did. You know no one has proven anything yet."
"Officer Morgan, she did. I know, don't ask questions, but I do know."
Was he a part of those who benefited from her efforts, or one of the snitches to help catch her? I wondered. I knew he is a Moor, and most of them are involved one way or another in all that goes down in this rat hole. They have the power, not the Melanics. The Moors and the Melanics were the majority of the African American prisoners, the Nuestra Familia, a Spanish American gang, represented a mere seven percent of the entire population, while the African Americans are the majority of 83 percent of the population. Whites and Asians made up the other 10 per cent.
"So, how do they do it?" I asked.

"Officer Morgan, you could, I mean not you but someone could put an awful lot of cocaine in a hollowed-out pen.
 One 'homie' would ask an Officer to borrow a pen, and of course would never give it back. It can be brought in a hollow lip stick case, the fold of a tie, in a woman's vagina."
I gave him a look to let him know he had gone a little too far.
"No offense to you officer, but you asked. "
"Alright, anything else?"
"Well, the men bring it in up their, you know, behind."
"Yuk."
Jerry laughed, "Ya, but there is a way, if it needs to be."
"Jerry, do you do this sort of thing?"
"You should know better to ask me something like that. Besides I'm a health freak, don't you see me run my miles everyday?"
"No, I hadn't noticed."
"Besides my African name tells you that I am not a warrior, I'm a peace maker."
I ignored his comment.
"How does the payment come?" I had a good idea how, but sometimes it is better to act as if you are not that aware of things that are apparent.
"Different ways, roll it back up and give it back in a hollow pen, send it through the mail or deliver it the same way as Officer Pluff got hers."
"I give, how did she get hers?"
"Girl, they met her right out the front door."

"You're kidding."
"It's the truth. I swear." He held up his hand, and had a very convincing expression on his face.

A few days later I was assigned to the back dock gun post and my phone rang.
"Back Post, officer Morgan speaking."
"Hi, Anne, dis' s DD, you won' believe da latest. De yard crew foun' dis' hole in da ground where someone was diggin' a tunnel from 'E' block. They were out dere lookin' at it during count time, da Sgt. and da yard crew."
"Geez, they never give up do they. They'd have to dig for an awful long time to get anywhere from that location. Ha ha."
DD laughed too, "I thought it was pretty stupid too, an' here's da res o' the gossip. Dis officer kept getting letters from a prisoner, finally she gave him her address at home so he could write her, 'cause she be afraid she would get caught like Pluff did. "
"Wait a minute, wait a minute, how did you find out about this?"
"She was just here on her lunch hour spilling her guts about it. She was upset, when she got her first letter, it was supposed to be a necklace enclosed. Instead it was pot rolled up tight with tape and listen to dis, a rubber over it."
"What?" I asked, "A rubber?" I could hardly keep from laughing.
"No joke, she was wantin' me to tell her what to do because today he asked her to bring it in."
"That's bad news. You know what I'd do don't you; I'd tell him it never came. Did she tell him it came?" I was more serious now.
"I don't know, I'll ask her when I can," she said.
"Wow, what a clinker, well, half time should be rolling around about now, it's going on eight o'clock, I'll talk to you later, okay DD? But, do call if you hear anything."
"I sure will, sister."

Chapter 14

My next day off the phone rang just as I was headed out the door.
"Hello?"
"Hi, Anne, it's Diane. What are you doing today? I need to talk to you."
"I was just headed out the door, going shopping. You know.... and we're talking right now."
"No, I mean not on the phone, this is serious. I want to look you in the eye when we speak."
I took a deep breath.
"Okay, do you want to come over here?"
"I can't, the kids are still sleeping. We could sit out on the deck to talk. I'll have the coffee ready."
"All right, I'll be there in a few minutes." I could get groceries after our talk, I thought as I backed out of the driveway. It was just a short drive to town.
Di had the coffee out and was sitting there waiting. While she poured the coffee, I perused the beauty of the day. Her flowers were all in bloom. Approaching the steps of the deck I said, "Hi."
"Sit down, Anne."
"Yes?" I asked.
"Have you been getting any overtime?"
"Uh-huh, but I work doubles so I can have my regular days off."
"I have been doing doubles too, they have been putting me everywhere. But, how do the officers treat you? I mean, do they, the officers, respect you?"
"Like how do you mean?" I wasn't ready to tell her about 'Officer-Grab-Me-and-Kiss-me-in-the-Dark.'
"Well, some of the officers I work with are helpful. If I have questions they are polite and answer them. But there are some who completely ignore me, they go on about their business and let me stand there feeling ignorant. You know, the prisoners pick up on that," Diane continued "I guess it's because I'm new and green when it comes to working on a different shift. Not knowing what has to be done."
"Hey," I interjected, "you are not green any more, just on the assignments you haven't done yet. I have felt 'green' from time to time, just let it go."
"You know last week I pulled a double and guess what the day officer had me do? " I asked her.
She shrugged her shoulders.

"Officer Clark said, 'go down and monitor showers.' Then Officer Bean said 'you going to send a woman to do that?' Then Officer 'Jack-Ass' came back with, 'she gets the same pay as we do, doesn't she?' So I went down and tried very hard to keep my eyes on their feet, looking for blood in case of a knifing."
'One time I actually looked up, cause I saw four feet pretty close. I couldn't believe what I saw. A penis and a set of tits bigger than mine!"
Diane laughed and said, "Ms. Jane. She locks on the gallery above mine, kind of keeps to the one predator, her mate. 'She's' really okay."
"Well, I have never seen anything like that in my entire life! Have you had to monitor showers?" I asked.
"Yes, I have, but I try to ignore them. I just make sure they get them, but not more than once daily. Making sure that they're not killing or fucking. Ms. Jane was in the process of a sex change when she got caught up into something, there was a fight, and she ended up being the only one alive. She had breast implants, and her cheeks were filled out."
"Well, she-he-it sure surprised me!" I said.
"Ms. Jane is harmless, it's the others that you need to look out for" said Diane.
"It's often that a critical incident could happen during showers. It's a time when there are approximately 15 –20 nude prisoners, with the exception of a towel and bar of soap. They can't really defend themselves against a predator. Many times it's an opportunity for someone to settle a grudge." I rolled into another story, continuing,
" One evening my partner and I let out 15 for showers. As they passed me I noticed one of them held his towel over his arm; it looked strange. Most times they would wrap the towel around their waist, and one over the shoulder. Dale and I were leaning on the railing, watching as they left the showers one at a time back to the gallery. All of a sudden that same guy, Reeves, took a shank and stabbed another inmate five times quicker than blinking your eyes.
Dale said, "Stay here," and he ran down from second gallery to base where the showers were on the east end. Two other officers at the desk ran towards the showers. Two more officers burst through the door from yard. Blood was all over the place. Radios shouted, 'Sticking in 'B' Block.'
BIG RED went off. Immediately all the loose prisoners hit the floor. Three of the officers tackled Reeves and cuffed him while the two yard officers took him to the 'hole' with just his towel covering his

ass; there was still snow on the ground. An ambulance took the 'victim' to the hospital. ... But this isn't what you asked me over for, so lets get to that."

Diane thought for a minute, and then began, "I had an experience last week when I was working overtime. My partner and I were assigned to the prison school. All we had to do was make rounds every so often and make sure everything was secure. He told me when the prisoners left we would have to sign their passes with the time and date, which allows the prisoner to get to their 'house' in only a few minutes. Otherwise they are 'out of place' a nice way of keeping security and order. If one or more went somewhere else it would show on the pass the time length, which is a means to monitor the time spent from the school to the block.

It was time for them to leave, we checked them out, signed passes, and they left," Diane continued.

"Then he said we would have to make a final round before we secured the building and left for the chow hall. He went one way and I the other, meeting at the center hallway. Coming around the corner I noticed him standing there with his pants unzipped and his penis hanging out. He asked me what I thought of it. I told him it was limp. He said to me, 'touch it, you know we don't have to go to the mess hall, we could get lost for two hours.' I told him, he could get lost, but I was going to the mess hall!" she concluded.

"Good for you! That's sickening and terrible. You know Diane it's strange that every time we are assigned to a new officer or new place, this sort of thing happens. I have heard it from others."

I was thinking about that time, when I was grabbed and kissed. No I still wasn't going to tell her. I asked myself why. Was I afraid what might happen if it gets out? Do I feel guilty for letting him get away with it? Do I feel that he thinks less of me because I didn't fight him off? I was worried about my life and safety. Sometimes it's just better to wait until it is necessary to tell.

Di said, " If I'm assigned with him again, I'm getting 'sick' and going home."

"Thank God for sick time, eh Diane?" I said trying to lighten the mood.

"There's one more thing that's bothering me. It seems strange that two officers were killed in the same year, from the same class, and officer Mayberry was friends with him, you know, did a lot with him during their academy."

"How do you know that?"

"Well, it's hearsay, but I heard his wife is a nut case and should have been put away a long time ago. Not to mention the dead female's husband."

"Are we talking about Don Mayberry, your friend? Di, don't work your brain overtime. Quit worrying. We have enough to keep our minds busy. It's time to go get my groceries, and other shopping done. Thanks for the coffee. Don't worry about 'limp dick,' you handled it right."

Diane grinned, "Yah."

"But, I will add that officers should be professional at all times; do their job, respect themselves and co-workers at all times. It reflects on their work performance and also shows a bad example to the prisoners. If you were assigned with him again I would tell him about this. See you at work."

" Okay. Bye," she said.

On the road my thoughts went to officer Stoner's murder. It was only eight months after officer Mayberry was murdered, in broad daylight, on the gallery. He didn't even see it coming, or so it seemed. I heard his wife was sick and had passed away. I felt bad, but kept telling myself it would not happen to me. Is there a conspiracy? Is there a connection?

My theory is that the 'old school guards' resented the 'new wave' officers, male and female alike. We took college educations to acquire the positions, where many of them came from the plough, unemployment line, or skid row to work. They used their brawn, beating the prisoner when they needed it. We used paper to maintain control. There had to be resentment.

There was resentment with some of the prisoners too. Once I was talking to a porter about that, and he said he liked it better before 'the new wave' came in to work. The prisoners were the one who unlocked the prisoners for chow, showers, etc. They were trusted more and had more freedom.

Where is the security in that? I thought. *They even did some of the paperwork. Was he delusional?*

Chapter 15

Another issue I feel needs attention, and should be brought to the new organizational meeting is the AIDS infected inmates. That's a definite case of unsafe conditions in the working place.

A fight broke out in the yard between two prisoners. A shank was drawn. The yard officer broke things up, fully aware that he could be cut. Later the officer found out one of the inmates is infected with AIDS. The officer feared he was infected during the scuffle. Not knowing much about this disease, he had to find out all he can to appease his fears. In some cases it takes up to five years to show up in a person's system.

I did some research on states laws and found that prisoners who test positive for AIDS are treated like any other inmate; they are not segregated from general population. If there is a misconduct issue, such as needle drugs or sexual contact, then the inmate will be put in Ad. Seg.

Another issue is that the officers were not told which inmate had AIDS. At that time, the union had some ideas like medical isolation, but never managed to enforce them.

The only thing that was practiced was screening all incoming prisoners. The percentage was 16 percent positive for AIDS, at the screening.

The state did not regularly test inmate population. The union was working to change that. The union wanted testing at least every six months for inmates who were knowingly infected with Al DS.

I never heard if the state had finally passed a law to protect the officers or inmates. Having the infected inmates tested every six months, and periodically testing the entire population would be a deterrent, and a form of protection.

I prepared topics to address at the next meeting. This one had priority over all others.

I sat in my living room recliner and read the application to join Better Conditions for Corrections Workers, which is a non-profit organization. Its purpose is to bring together individuals (male and female) who share the basic belief of advocating for the enforcement of sexual harassment policies, and state and federal laws prohibiting sexual harassment in the workplace.

The group also works to enforce laws and provide assistance to personnel, with any personal or substance abuse problems.

In my opinion it was a personal vendetta against the experiences that happened to a selective whimpering society. Of course it was only my opinion, I had had so many harassment issues to date that they became second to other more serious issues.

So, where does AIDS come into the two topics?

I never did join, but I still have the application in case I change my mind. I did attend a couple more sessions though, only to see if their purpose had expanded to something more than personal problems.

We were working in a place where our lives were at stake every minute of every hour. I felt their personal problems were a secondary topic on my list.

It's funny though, after the DW attended and found out what the purpose of the organization was, we were educated on sexual harassment at work. We were taken into a classroom near the control center, and given papers explaining the two examples of sexual harassment.

"One is Quid Pro Quo, which means if you do this then I'll do that," Sgt. Ward said.

"The second is undesirable conversation between two people. Or, there could be a third party who overheard it and it also could be applied to that rule."

"How can this type of incident be corrected?" one officer asked.

Sgt. Ward answered, "Write-ups and reprimands. For instance, if two officers are exchanging an unsavory joke, and a female officer overhears it and becomes offended by the tainted conversation, she may press sexual harassment charges against the two officers. They may not even know that she could hear them talking."

If we ever needed to talk to anyone Sgt. Ward would be very attentive and give us any assistance needed.

Just be professional, folks! Then this will never happen!

The Saturday, March 24, 1990 issue of the Evening Journal, headline read 'Prison Group Fights Sexual Harassment.'

Female prison employees formed a group and hope to be instrumental in fighting sexual harassment on the job.

About 25 workers from various the state prisons formed Better Working Conditions for Corrections Officers. Officers in Dover Hills and Oxford prisons have expressed interest in joining.

The organization is made of female officers, psychologists and a staff sergeant, and is intended to provide support to women and men who believe they have been sexually harassed. The workers may pursue a transfer or disciplinary action against the offender.

Group Coordinator Diane Collins said women fear retaliation from male co-workers if they file complaints, and may have difficulty proving allegations because officials want proof.

"That makes no sense. If someone wanted to assault me, he wouldn't wait until someone was watching," Collins said.

Collins, a former corrections officer at Johnstown Prison and now employed at Higginsdale, started the group after filing harassment charges against a co-worker.

Jesse Hernandez was acquitted of administrative and legal charges that he grabbed Collins and tried to kiss her. The Maplewood man is now suing her for liable.

Collins, of the Johnstown area, said she lost her case because there were no witnesses.

Carrie Lancelot, the Department of Corrections sexual harassment coordinator, said the department couldn't accept the word of one employee against another.

Dismissed complaints are recorded and could help build a file on someone, she noted.

Lancelot's job and others addressing harassment were created since 1987, when corrections officer Cheryl Mayberry was assaulted and killed at the Johnstown prison.

Lancelot attributes increased complaints statewide to better education efforts.

In 1989, 160 complaints were filed statewide. As of January, 17 had resulted in disciplinary action; 37 resulted in an action, such as training or counseling; 44 were dismissed; and 54 are pending, she said.

Finally someone heard, and action is being taken. I didn't have a witness so I felt it would do exactly nothing to submit a complaint. I feel for Diane, more since I read the article. I believe the retaliation would be more severe if the offender were transferred, or dismissed. The offender had to have a serious emotional problem to be so insecure and need to boost their ego, and boast their achievements. Not telling saved me from possible death, but death was all around each officer who worked here.

Chapter 16

"Officer Morgan, report to the control center," the loudspeaker spouted. I was working the chow lines.
Sgt. Ward, an attentive woman who cared about sexual harassment and the female workers, was waiting for me in the center of the marble floored room. She talked in low tones to the Captain who stood beside her. They looked up when I walked in.
"Hi, Morgan, I want you to go with Sgt. Ward to the prison school. Gather the teachers and the librarian Vivian Green into one room and talk to them about the security that the officers offer to them, and also tell them why they should not trust the prisoner."
"Do you mind if I ask why you chose me?" I asked.
"No I don't, you have worked there, you have the experience with that inmate hiding behind the piano that time, just relate to them how you felt, and how this can be avoided," the Captain said.
"Okay, I'll do my best."
"I know, that's why I asked you. You know Sgt. Ward here don't you? She is the co-coordinator for sexual harassment."
"Yes, briefly, we have talked once at the meeting a few years ago," I said.
We walked to the school saying very little. I decided Sgt. Ward could assemble the women, and I would do the talking. When we were almost to the school area, I took a minute to tell her my plan and checked to see if it was all right with her. She agreed. She could add anything that I might forget.
I went into the empty room and waited. When everyone was in the room I closed the door and began.
"Hello. For those of you that do not know me, I am officer Morgan, and this is Sgt. Ward. Sgt. Ward is the sexual harassment co-coordinator for this complex. I'm going to tell you something that you may already know in part, but the Captain and Sgt. Ward both feel it is necessary for you all to know about," I continued.
"About three months ago, there was a prisoner who did not leave when the prisoners were ordered back to the block. It was right about this time of the day. The building should have been cleared of any prisoners. He hid behind the piano, waiting for the teachers to leave. He had one thing on his mind; to rape one of you. Not knowing what happened after prisoner movement was over, he wasn't aware that the two officers on duty would do their rounds, checking everywhere. This day in particular, the officer had a hunch, went into the room where the piano was and started to shake it down. There were several

cardboard boxes behind the piano, and the prisoner was under them. When the officer came closer to the piano, the prisoner jumped up and ran past the officer out on to the block. This officer I'm speaking of was myself. I was covering for an officer who called in sick. The prisoner wasn't able to complete his mission this time, but that doesn't mean there could be another time."

I looked at the librarian, and she was grinning.

The little fool, she was up to something. Perhaps the Captain knew or suspected her.

"I ran after him," I continued, " my partner following, directly behind me. We found him in his cell, and afterward wrote him up for being out of place. It could have been written as an attempted escape, but we settled for an out-of-place ticket. Be warned folks, these guys are in here because they did more than sing off key in church. This particular prisoner is in for the third time for habitual rape."

"Why? He is so nice, it is hard to believe that he would try to rape me, I'm sixty years old," said one of the teachers.

"Okay, just for your information, the last woman he raped was in her eighties, with tits hanging down so far the only thing between them was her belly button."

No response.

The librarian, Vivian Green, was still grinning. She must have a crush on one of them, the fool.

Sgt. Ward added, "Rapist do not care, all they are thinking is that they need sex. They need to feel they are in control. They want to see a woman submit to their force. Remember one thing; the prisoner doesn't care if you are ugly, short, fat, tall, skinny, young, or old. The only thing they want is sex. They will rape you, if given a chance."

"Okay, do you have any questions, or comments?" I asked.

"Well, I have a porter, and he is safe. I can trust him. He said he'd protect me if it was necessary," the librarian said.

"If you believe that, you are in trouble. In here you can trust no one. No one. I'd hate to come on shift to hear that one of you were raped, and killed. Four years ago a female officer was killed right below us in the auditorium. I cannot be more emphatic when I say that you cannot trust anyone in here. As for the porter that says that he will take care of you," I said looking at the librarian. " From what I was taught in inter-communications class, what he really was saying is that he would take care of you if you took care of him. A con always expects something in return. There are few exceptions," I concluded.

"Oh, I never thought about that!" said the librarian.

"Well, just be careful, and be alert at all times. Are there anymore questions?" No one responded. " Sgt. Ward, do you have anything to add?" I asked.

"No, you pretty well covered it. But I do want you girls to remember that if you need sexual harassment counseling, feel free to call me or let the Captain know, and I will get with you as soon as possible."

" That's all for now, and thank you for staying over for this half hour." I said.

The Sgt. thanked me for helping, and I thanked her for her input. We parted at the cross-corridor gates.

I continued to wonder about the librarian. I hoped I'd never hear that she was caught up in a situation she couldn't get away from.

Chapter 17

A few weeks later I was assigned to the gate between the blocks and the outer buildings; which included the dining room, auditorium, yard, chapel, industries and the back gate where the trucks came in with supplies. Industries buildings were a collection of several buildings on about a two-acre plot.

Behind the buildings, the prisoners have a five-acre garden, where they work each day during growing season. This was where the sun stayed the longest without the shadows of the 20-foot prison walls. Most of the garden had been harvested by this time of year. Vegetables grown in the garden were used in the prisoners' meals.

It was fall, the time of year when it is dark by eight o'clock. I was on the back post watching the yard. This post had the best vantage point for full observance, although two more manned posts along the wall also helped.

There are basketball hoops, and courts. Some prisoners were playing, many stood by the side watching. Off in the corner there was some tattoo action the yard crew seemed to overlook. I felt tattooing was another way to contract AIDS. Other prisoners were at the baseball diamond playing a game, some sat in circles singing, another group practiced karate or some other form of self-defense. Others used the fence as a guide to run around and get their miles in. Pacing them so as to not be exhausted, just stay in shape.

All of a sudden a fight broke out on the basketball court. Fists were flying, and a shank came out. The gleaming steel flashing my way jolted me into action. I ran from my shack post and racked a shell in my 233-bolt action rifle. The sound of it echoed across the entire yard, bringing total silence, and all looked my way. The yard crew was running in the direction of the basketball courts, the fight broke up; two were ushered off the court and straight to administrative segregation.

No one was injured, so it wasn't necessary to call for an ambulance. Things quieted up quickly. Everything was under control.

I returned to my post, removed the shell from the chamber, and placed the rifle next to the shotgun. When I began writing in the logbook about the incident the telephone rang.

"Gun post three, Officer Morgan speaking."
"You should have shot!"
"I didn't think it was necessary," I said.
"Well, you should have. "
"Who is this?"

"Officer Sobalesky."
"Oh, where are you assigned tonight?"
"In the Prison School."
"So you aren't in the yard, so what do you have, periscope eyes Sobalesky?"
"No but I heard the radio transactions, and you should have shot."
"But, I didn't," I said. I hung up.
This was definitely harassment; he was on the other side of the prison.
"15 to Sgt. Hall" I said into my radio.
"This is Hall."
"Please TX me when you can."
"Copy"
It only took a couple minutes when the phone rang.
"Three Post, Officer Morgan," I answered.
"What was it you wanted?" Sgt. Hall asked.
"I had a call reprimanding me for not shooting. Just a co-worker, not the Captain."
"Officer Morgan, it didn't warrant a warning shot,"
"I didn't think so, thanks Sgt."
"That's Okay."
This was the judgment call that my Sgt. in the academy talked about. No one would know unless they experience it personally. Only then will you have to decide to use your judgment and act in a fraction of a second.

Officer North left for work early, he received a call to stop in at the warden's office around noon to talk to Warden Hale.
North knew it was coming. He passed the academy without effort. Today he was unsure what the call was.
He drove with his back to the sun heading west towards the prison.
The warden's office was in a separate building near the highway.
North pulled into the parking lot noting that only four vehicles were parked. The fewer the better, he didn't want too many witnesses to his visit. North was secretive about his life.
His secretary greeted him, "Hello, how may I help you?"
"I have an appointment with Warden Hale," he said.
"Are you officer North?" she asked.
"Yes."
"I'll let him know you are here."

She entered Hales' office and closed the door.
Within seconds she returned and said, " You may go in now."

"Hello, North, how are you doing? I have checked your background, and find you were a pilot in the Marines."
"Yes, that is true," North said.
"I have called you in to discuss a transfer."
"Transfer?"
"Yes, it will look as though you are transferring to another prison, however I have another job for you," the warden continued, "I would like you to do some flying for me. After checking your credentials, I am sure you are the man for this job. The pay is good. Better than the state job."
"How much better?" North asked.
"Let's say that you will not want for anything. No questions asked, just do the flight when I schedule it, and contact you."
North thought a minute. He loved flying. He was getting older, and the opportunity to move on before retirement sounded good.
"Alright, when will you put the transfer in?" he asked.
"One week, your last day will be Friday." Warden Hale said.
"Okay," said officer North.
"Do you have any more questions? I won't tell you the particulars on your flights until the that day."
"No, I will wait until then," said officer North.
"Until then. You were in to see about an transfer, if anyone saw you here."
"Right."
Something tells me this job will not be crop dusting, officer North thought as he descended the steps from the wardens' office.

Working in the Chow Hall was really easy, but it could be dangerous. It would take about two and-a-half-hours out of the evening schedule. The predators always were taking the food away from an older or a sissy inmate. Sometimes the Mores would plan a knifing, which is easily covered up in all the prison movement. We always had to be alert, and ready to react to any given incident. When they were finished eating we would go to the front of the dining room near the

food lines and start pushing them out. Not physically, but forming a line of about three or four officers, saying 'Time's up, time to go' inching our way to the back of the dining room as one at a time would get up and leave in the direction of the exit doors.
Officer Davis stood near me, grinning his usual grin. He leaned near my ear and asked me,
"Do you swallow?"
"I'm going to pretend I didn't hear that," I pressed my lips thin.
"Oh, I'm sorry."
"You had better be, I thought you were a gentleman."
"I am."
I let it go, was this sexual harassment? You bet it was. Quid Pro Quo, or undesirable conversation, which of the two categories was this? It definitely was undesirable to me.

You know, he always treated me like a lady at first, and an officer after that. I always respected him and his work.

He saved a prisoner's life once by sticking his finger in the bleeding hole where a shank had been. He definitely was a good officer.
I was relieved when he refrained from using undesirable language in front of me after that.

Arriving at work one day, Captain Wiggins told me to go straight to the arsenal and get a pistol. I was told to take a state car to the Hospital downtown to stand guard.
Prisoner Robinson had been sliced across the neck and was at emergency there. The captain assumed that they were going for his jugular but missed. I was to relieve the day shift officer that was already there.
"You will be taking O. Johnston with you."
"Yes, sir. Thank you."

Officer Johnston is a housing officer and not pistol qualified. He told the officer in the arsenal he wouldn't need a pistol, but would take extra leg irons along in case we had to bring the inmate back.
I was impressed. 'Good looking out.' I thought.
We arrived at the emergency room about 30 minutes later. The officer in charge was impatient to get off shift and go home.
"It's about time you got here," he said. He was a wiry looking little man, named Stanley Hoynojski.
"Okay, brief us, so you can get out of here."

"Well, it's like they told you. This inmate was walking back from the chow hall, when three prisoners jumped him. Two held him while the other quickly sliced him across the back of his neck and laid it open. The yard crew was upon him in seconds. The three they disappeared in the crowd, but we will find out later who did it. There's enough snitches in there, someone will tell for a favor."

"What time was it when this happened?" I asked.

"Around 12:30."

"Has anyone seen him yet?" Officer Johnson asked.

"Naw, they just put a gauze pad over it for now. Hey, I better get out of here. Thanks, and good luck."

"Thanks."

I suppose they will take care of civilians first and then the state inmate.

After what seemed an eternity, a nurse came into the screened off area at 4:15. She picked up the clipboard, glanced at the information on the sheet, and said,

"This prisoner will have to have an ex-ray and a MRI, to see if there is any nerve damage."

Not knowing anything about medical terminology, I smiled and said, " Okay."

The big inmate had a very thick neck. He was muscular not overweight. The gash was about four inches long making a gap that was more than an inch wide. The gap was swollen and appeared to lay open.

I could understand the question that there may be nerve damage. The wound was deep too. I was surprised that the bleeding had stopped and the wound was just oozing.

First we went to the ex-ray department, down the hall and to the north part of the hospital. We waited there in a small area, for the prisoners turn. An hour-and-a-half went by.

He sat there with his eyes closed. I knew he was in pain.

While Robinson was being ex-rayed, I stood near with a protective apron on, in case, but I was sure he wouldn't try anything. He was hurting, even though he never let a sound out of him.

Officer Johnston and I made small talk to pass time. He was a good officer, I had worked with him before, and I thought a lot of his work performance.

"Officer Johnston, you really have impressed me with your work performance."

"Thank you." He looked at me as if he was surprised that I would come right out and say it to him. "This is a serious injury, isn't it?"

"Yes, he'll probably have to go into P.C. when he heals."
"Wonder what he did to get it."
"In there, it could be anything."
Finally the ex-ray was completed; it was back to the little partition to wait for the MRI. The waiting area was screened and separated with hanging sheets. I couldn't help but believe that we were overlooked, because the time was dragging. Then the hospital shift change took a few more minutes. It was sixish when the MRI attendant came with a stretcher to wheel Robinson down the corridor towards MRI. I felt every pain he went through, going in and being still so the pictures took.
It was done very quickly. We returned to the waiting space in emergency.
A doctor arrived at 8:30pm. He briskly asked, "Have you been here long?"
Johnston and I looked at each other.
"No, just since two o'clock," Johnson and I replied.
"Well, this won't take long, all I have to do is sew him up and he can return to, ...well maybe we'll take him upstairs for a day or two to for observation. Have you been there before?"
"Yes, once, I came over and brought a prisoner back after he recovered from surgery."
When the doctor started to sew him up, at the third stitch the inmate jerked, and the needle stuck into the doctors' hand.
"Do YOU have AIDS?" the doctor asked in a loud irritated voice.
"NO! Do you?" replied the inmate in the same loud voice.
I held my breath, cupped my hand over my mouth, this could be serious for the doctor.

It was 9:30 by the time we escorted the prisoner upstairs to the Prison wing. This area was secured, very much like the prison. Guards everywhere.
My concern was for the doctor, everything else went quite well.

Chapter 18

I had been watching a certain female officer for almost three years. Not the one the ADW asked me to watch. Officer Bronson has worked at the same locations as I have, noticing her notes in the log, gave me some insight on how she worked. When her actions were note worthy, I would enter them in my personal notebook at home.

About a month earlier I was on assignment at the cross corridor gates, when this particular officer came from her assignment and instead of going directly to the control center, she used her pass key to gain access to the South Complex, which is against the policy. She started to talk to one of the yard porters. The conversation lasted approximately 15 minutes. She kept looking at her watch and glancing in my direction. The two of them talked in undertones which made it impossible to hear any of the conversation. She looked into his eyes from time to time, which indicating to me, her sincerity.

Many questions entered my mind as I replayed the scenario. What was she doing there instead of her assignment? What excuse did she make to leave the block? Did she get permission or did she just leave without saying anything?

The facts were these: it was obvious her destination was to see that particular prisoner. She went nowhere else, made contact and returned to her assignment all in about fifteen minutes.

Two weeks later, I was on the same assignment. As the evening drew neigh, she came through again. She walked through the north gate, locked it, then went through the south gate, stopped dead in her tracks, and asked,

" Is the bathroom working down the sub hall?"

I answered, "Yes."

She went down the sub hall to the bathroom. Soon after, the same prisoner who talked to her the last time came up to the south gate and asked me if I had seen Ms. Bronson.

I replied, "She went down to the bathroom."

He said, "Okay," and hung around until she came out.

I was relieved for a 15-minute break before she came out. The relief officer, Watkins, arrived and I made a quick decision to tell him to watch her and let me know if she passed anything to the porter. I also told him not to ask any questions.

When I returned from break, he told me she spoke to the prisoner and then went out to the south end of the hall into the south complex. He said she was there for a few minutes with the porter, she returned to the north side leaving the prisoner. I thanked him. I'm sure he knew what I was thinking, but I didn't elaborate or explain at that point.

I thought about it briefly and decided to call one of my friends in the yard.

"I need a positive identification on the yard porter. I saw something that I need to document, in case I need it in the future."

He said he'd get back with me.

A few minutes later he called and said the prisoner was Ferguson #354986, in 'D' Block. He advised me to tell the Control Sergeant and tell him everything. I called the Sgt. and asked him if he could come down to speak to me. I told him what took place, but no names. He wanted me to write a memo.

"Do you know who this prisoner is?"

"I know his name, that's all." I produced a slip of paper with his name and number on it.

He glanced at the paper with an expression that made me think he already knew who it was.

"He's that prisoner who slit a hostage's throat a while back. You know we don't do much when it is a prisoner. They all have to go one way or another. We have him where we can watch him. That's why he has the yard working job."

"I didn't know about that, Sgt., I won't write a memo at this time. I just thought you should know about this in case something happens in the future."

"There's not much I can do about this if you don't write a memo."

Sgt. Jones looked at me with a slightly disgusted expression, turned on his heel and walked back to the control center.

I realized that I should have kept this to myself. The ADW only asked me to watch Officer Julia Brown; no one else, but I had seen a lot since I started working. The female officer Brown definitely was 'dirt.' She was 'muling' dope in, but anyone could be the 'brains' behind the mule. Even the Sergeant I talked to. I knew then, that I had to keep my mouth shut. I mention it to anyone again. Just do the job, go home and live a life away from this place, go to church Sunday when it is possible, spend time with my children and Ralph when he was home, just be normal. I would add Sgt. Jones' attitude, everything in my journal.

Chapter 19

Samuel Goldberg, the District Manager for Acme Accidental Death and Casualty Insurance Company, was due to arrive at the Acme Accidental Death and Casualty Insurance Company's branch office between ten and eleven o'clock. This insurance company had the contract with the Department of Corrections.

The Easterburg branch office was mainly ran by Max Idleman, although he had three good helpers, and a reliable secretary. Max sat eagerly awaiting the arrival of Mr. Goldberg; there were a few things he had to discuss with him, especially the Mayberry case. He reviewed the file placed before him by his secretary, Marie. A fresh mental picture of the facts would enable him to present them to Sam.

Max took great care dressing this morning. He selected his dark gray suit, white shirt, and light blue tie. The thinning dark brown hair left a ring, leaving a shine through a few strands on top. For mid-forties he was at least fifty pounds over weight, so in spite of his attempts to look good, he appeared sloppy. He sat nervously watching his watch, glancing from the door to the file before him, wondering what Sam would suggest that he do next with the Mayberry case.

He noticed a shadow through the frosted window at the door, and immediately knew it was Mr. Goldberg. He rose to his feet, hand outstretched to greet Sam.

"Hi, Sam, good to see you. How are the wife and family?"

"Oh, fine, fine," Sam answered, he wasn't about to tell him that his marriage was getting pretty shaky, what with all the long hours away from home and he being twenty years her senior. Sam is taller than Max by four inches or so and carried his weight well. He removed the tan colored trench coat revealing a remarkably well-dressed man in a dark navy pinstripe suit, accented with a burgundy colored tie.

Max thought Sam was the picture of success. He cleared his throat and began.

"Have a seat Sam, can I get you some coffee?"

"Sure; black."

"Marie…" Max said.

"Got it." Marie said.

" I have the files you asked for here, but the main topic is this Mayberry case," Max began.

Samuel frowned slightly and said, "Brief me again, will you Max, there are so many."

"Okay, this is the one where the woman was killed in the prison. A lifer inmate was blamed for the murder. It should have been a closed case, but other evidence came up that led me to suspect the husband."

"Alright, and that was because the husband could inherit a great wealth from his first marriage if he wasn't remarried at the time of his ex-father-in-law's death," Sam remembered.

"Correct," Max said. "Moreover, I found that Mr. Mayberry has purchased a beautiful home in the country, with a swimming pool and all the trimmings. I peeked in the shed and there was an antique 1934 Ford Coupe that he was working on. At the time of Mrs. Mayberry's death they were living in town in a dingy apartment. I also discovered that his first wife, who is also deceased, was from the Dumont Dynasty, we're talking millions of dollars here!"

"No shit!" Sam thought a minute, "Is there anything else you can add to this information?"

"Only that he has a weakness for the old life. He likes to party, and gamble. My man has seen him at the tracks on several different occasions."

"So, on what little income he lives on, it's obvious he is expecting a lot more money to back up his life style?"

"Obviously!" Max said.

"Well," Sam paused and pursed his lips a moment. "Let's put a decision on hold for now, and keep the investigation going."

"But, in all due respect, it's been almost three years since her death…" Max's voice trailed off.

"I don't give a damn if its ten years, we aren't paying off until I'm satisfied that the state is liable. Don't forget that this is where we get our paycheck." Sam's fist hit the desk with a loud slam.

"Okay, okay, okay. So what do I tell him when he calls is?" Max choked out the words.

"Calm down. Just tell him that we have a thorough investigation going on, and when we are satisfied with all the evidence, he will hear from us," Sam concluded.

"Good enough. Oh, here are those files you want to take with you. It's close to lunch, would you like to join me at the café across the street before you head out?"

"Not this time, Max, but thanks just the same. I have to be in Belton by two o'clock," Sam said.

No wonder he keeps in shape Max thought as he shuffled down the block to his favorite restaurant.

Chapter 20

Jonesy was transferred to another prison. My last conversation with him was about officer Robinson, the arrogant one, who stole from the prisoners.

I remember him laughingly say, "I told you I'd take care of it. He be playin' us He need a lesson. We have a way of takin' care o' anyone who helps themselves to others property. He took my buddies supply. You know what I mean?"

The eyes knew. The eyes were the prisoners, a people who had all the time in the world to watch us when we were watching them.

Jonesy told me when the sergeant took Robinson into the office to question Robinson, he unzipped his fly and yelled, 'So you wanna see my dick mother-fucker, well here it is'. He yelled it so loud anyone nearby heard it.

Jonesy told it all.

He was transferred out, I never saw him again. It was good that he was gone, for every inmate transferred to another prison, another was sent to fill the empty cell. It was a good system, kept them rotated, and not too accustomed to what was happening.

Diane was right when she said that Prison only restrains criminals temporarily. Most will return to our communities to prey on society. Although the return rate was 87% at that time, I have heard that it has lowered some in the twenty some years that has passed.

We needed to realize, that unless we help criminals learn to think differently, they would continue to prey upon us. A criminal is rational, calculating and deliberate in their actions. They know right from wrong, but believe whatever they are doing is 'right' for them. Prisons are a breeding ground for crime. No criminal wants to return to prison and no criminal expects to.

Stress, not physical injury is the greatest occupational hazard to people working in corrections. New correctional employees enter into the prisons, eager to do a good job. The environment is totally 'alien' to them. Your gut feeling tells you what to do and how to handle each situation, but administration and seasoned officers have their own theory for the best possible results. It takes time and experience to come to realize that not all personnel think and feel the same. Some become cynical or indifferent to all occasions. Some quit the job, or transfer to another prison, or become promoted to a "softer" job; meaning less stress.

I'm grateful for Diane's input; it helped me think a little straighter, and not so guilty when I wasn't thinking the same as the administration.

Chapter 21

Ole Johnston was the local gas station owner. He also had a mechanic, Bob, on duty. The additional service helped keep the gas price down.

Ole is liked by most of the town's people. He puffs his cigar and always had a comment to say about any subject. Oles' grandfather, George H. Johnston, came from Scotland and settled in Johnstown in the late 1870's. The town grew from a one-horse town to a 30,000 populace. The town is named after his grandfather.

Although Ole was slight built, he stood 5' 11" tall and carried himself well. He isn't really handsome; dark hair and brown eyes, good complexion making him look younger than his 49 years. He is married to a sweet woman and has three lovely daughters. However this didn't stop the teenage girls from hanging at the station and flirting with him. They like his happy-go-lucky personality.

One day a truck rolled into the station and pulled up to the pumps. The driver was so irate that he jumped out of the truck before Ole had time to get there to pump his gas.

"Howdy son, how are you today? Fill her up?" Olee asked.

"I have a problem, this truck is full of chickens on ice in wooden crates and it's too late to get into the prison to deliver them."

Ole kept pumping, with a small grin on his face. "Sorry to hear that buddy, but how many of those crates of chicken will you give me if I can get you through the back gate and get your chicken delivered to the prison mess hall?"

"Will a couple do?"

"You betcha. Hold up then, while I make a phone call." Ole hung the gas nozzle in place and went into the gas station for the phone.

"Hi, is the warden in?" …. "Well put him on.".… "Hey Mike, I have a delivery truck headed your way with a load of chicken on ice for tomorrows dinner, can you make an exception to the time and let him in?"

"Sure, I wondered where it was, we've been waiting for him. Just ride with him and I'll have the yard sergeant and two others meet you at the gate." Said the Warden.

"Okay Mike, consider the deed done. See you in a little while."

"Hey, Bob," he yelled to his mechanic. "Cover for me a few minutes while I go with this guy. It won't take more than a few minutes."

"That's alright Olee take all the time you need," Bob said. Olee was good to Bob he took him in when he needed a job, Bob, Ole's cousin, lived with him and his family until he could get back on his feet again.

Ole jumped up into the truck, lit his cigar and said, "By Gawd, we'll have chicken for supper tonight!"

"Hello, Captain Wiggins, this is the warden. I need you to get someone down to the back gate to let a delivery full of chicken in."

"Got it," Captain Wiggins said.

"Thank you." The warden hung up and smiled to himself.

"Control center to Sgt. Hall, take two officers to the back gate to let a truck of chicken in."

"Copy."

When the Sgt. asked officer Porter and me to meet him at the back gate I knew something was up. I opened the large 20-foot high gats with a push of a button so the truck could get in. I did the paperwork, noted in the logbook the time and license plate number.

The truck stopped, and the driver waited until the officers waved the long-handled mirrors under the truck, checking for contraband. It was routine to do a complete search each time a truck entered through the back gate. Some of the drivers were impatient, but seasoned ones just waited.

Hey, that's Ole Johnston with him, what's going on? Never mind, Anne, you do not need to know, you have your assignment and that's enough. But, Ole Johnston? His cousin Herbert Johnston works in the prison, he went with me on a run once. I wonder if that's why he's here?

A reception committee of Sergeant Kincaid, two officers from the loading dock, and the warden met the truckload of chicken! I suppose it would be easier for the warden to be there when the truck arrived since it was an unusual event. The Captain escorted the warden.

Although I was told to watch officer Julia Brown, I felt I should note how unusual it was the warden met the chicken truck. Was there something with the chicken?

I haven't really seen officer Brown a whole lot. I only know she is very attractive, and has a slightly snobbish demeanor. She keeps to herself at roll call. I would watch who she stood near, and talked to during that 15-minute daily briefing.

Being in custody, while she was in housing made it hard to really know where she went, whom she talked to. I planned to talk to the DW and ask her about going into housing to watch officer Brown a little closer. I really didn't want to have that close of contact with the inmates. It was better for me to be able to breath outdoors, even though the weather could be rough in the winter. The smell in the blocks hits you immediately; it smells like several hundred toilets flushing at the same time, homemade cigarette smoke, paper fires used to cook food over the toilet, and body odor.

The first time I actually saw officer Julia Brown was from my roof post in the early spring. My assignment was over the Chow Hall door and along the roof to the checkpoint gate.

She came out of 'A' Block and at first I believed she was going to monitor the prisoners in the chow hall; usually at least two officers from each block would help. She walked down the sidewalk, and stopped to talk to one of the prisoners, leaning against the cyclone woven fence.

Did I see that or was it my imagination that she touched his hand? This wouldn't be the first time I saw an officer touch a prisoner. I remember when one of my senior officers actually touched the prisoner with both hands on his shoulders. She's now working in the north complex as Sgt.

The chow lines hadn't started yet so I could slowly walk along the edge of the roof watching where officer Brown went. Obviously she wasn't going into the Officers Dining Room, or the Chow Hall. She walked up to the checkpoint gate, through the door, and stopped to look back at the yard to make sure no one saw her. She obviously didn't look up, or she would have seen me looking down.

I quickly scampered across to see if she went out the south gate to the southern complex. I knew I shouldn't be that far from my post, but I could say I needed to use the bathroom, if anyone asked. Sure enough, she came out the other side and walked straight up to a prisoner I had never seen before. He was remarkably handsome; a light skinned African American, and golden hair. It would be easy to find out who he was, and where his cell was.

She took her hand out of her pocket and gave him something. He took it, but did not give her anything in return. Was it possible that she would be paid later, in the sane manner that O. Pluff was?

I'd better get back to my post. Don't want to arouse suspicion. Only the DW can know what I just observed. It must be something more substantial.

Sitting in my 'shack', I realized it took officer Brown a little longer to arrive back also. She must have gone to the control center or used the restroom. I really didn't feel right watching her. So far she really hadn't done anything I could document.

She came out of the Officers Dining Room; she must have used her passkey to enter from the kitchen corridor. She didn't stop to talk to her connection near the yard passing as if she didn't even know him. Didn't she feel responsible for an inmates where a bouts?

Why was he still there, when chow lines were going to start? This really was suspicious. I wonder if she realizes that the sky has eyes. She should have asked him why he wasn't in the block, this was an 'out-of-place' infraction.

When I arrived home that night it was just after eleven, I went directly to the desk. I kept my journal in the third drawer. I wrote all that I saw today including officers Browns little escapade. I also made a note about the chicken and the warden at the loading dock at the kitchen. I was finished writing in my journal, had a little snack and watch TV until I wound down before bed.

"Hey, Mike. I'm going back up to the control center, so we can wrap this shift up" the Captain said.

"Sure, Captain, I'll stay here for a few more minutes," the warden said. When Captain Wiggins was out of hearing range he continued.

"Grab the two crates with the red writing on them, Kincaid, and bring them into the office."

Kincaid gave him a knowing look and proceeded to place the two in his office. The remaining load went into the coolers. Ole and the driver helped unload the chicken. Between the three the load was off, and the driver was ready to proceed to the back gate and off prison property.

Ole was looking forward to his chicken back at the station. They drove off towards the back gate where the yard crew was waiting for them to return. With very little effort the truck was gone and driving downtown to the gas station.

He jumped down from the truck and yelled, "Thanks, for the ride, buddy. See you next time."

Bob the mechanic came out, grinning and scratching his dark brown curly hair.

Back in the office, the warden and Kincaid were pulling plastic bags out of the cavity of each chicken. Neatly stacking them into a duffle bag, to be transported to the warden's office later.

They both were grinning and mentally counting the money.

Chapter 22

When I arrived at work, sirens were blowing non-stop. Everyone was buzzing about day's events, three inmates had escaped. They escaped through industries, a group of buildings that made state furniture. The furniture made in industries is used in Secretary of State, unemployment, and social service offices. The three escapees were missed at noon count.

The Captain came out of his office and stood on the steps.

"Listen up folks, there has been an escape. Three inmates have been planning this for quite some time. We think they went through the tunnels from industries towards the east wall where they went out the back towards the southeast side.

The three hiding in the bushes jumped two officers who were making a routine round in a state jeep checking the outside perimeter. Inmates, Gus Alsocost, Wilhelm Schlatske, and Stanley Bolkovicz, jumped from the bushes and forced officers Joe Maloney and Kenny Whycliff, to drive them off the prison property. The officers were pushed out the moving vehicle.

"How did they force them to do this?" I heard someone ask.

"With this," he held up what looked like a 38 revolver. The captain continued, "Look at it closely folks, because this is what you are supposed to be looking for when you do routine shakedowns. One of the three had this hand-made gun for some time now. They made it with soap, and dyed it black with shoe dye from industries. It fell on the ground when they pushed the officers out of the jeep. There are roadblocks from here to Allentown, a 70-mile distance from the prison, they won't be getting too far. In the meanwhile, you are going to do a complete shakedown of the entire prison. If you see anything, I mean anything, that looks slightly suspicious, let me know immediately." He paused a minute to confer with the Lieutenant, who handed him a sheet of paper. Captain Wiggins cleared his throat and continued.

"We will divide up into five groups, the following will go with Sgt. Johnston to 'A' Block, ..."

I was in the first group, and couldn't hear the rest of the assignments. The prison was under total lockdown and the inmates were yelling and making all kinds of noise. All prison traffic was concluded right after the sirens started. The first shift had immediately cleared the library, school, industries, chapel, and chow hall. All the prisoners were locked in their cell, within approximately 25 minutes.

The first cells checked out were the kitchen prison worker cells; otherwise we could have a riot if the prisoners couldn't eat. I was assigned to fourth gallery east side. My partner was Gillman, a neat guy to work with, sensible, professional, with a good sense of humor, which helped the day go by easier.

"Put your back against the bars please, we are doing a complete shake down," I said and the prisoner complied. Officer Gillman cuffed him and I keyed open his cell door.

Gillman watched the prisoner while I searched his cell. In the very first cell, I found a fake identification card. I put it in the front pocket of my shirt, finished the shakedown and let the inmate back in his cell. I nodded to Gillman and we went on the bulkhead, there I showed him the I.D.

"Look at this," I said

"Bingo! We need to take it to the Captain."

"We can as soon as he arrives here, I heard him say that he would make his rounds, starting here," I said.

"Okay, I'll do the next cell. You watch, I want to find something too," officer Gillman chided.

Gillhead was a 'trip,' his antics tickled me pink making me laugh.

We kept searching cells, but didn't find much. I bet if there was anything, it was burned, thrown through the catwalk vents or down on base before we arrived at their cell. We could hear the tinkling of steel falling down into the catwalks, so we knew that some of us would have to retrieve the shanks that were thrown out later. I also believe that the first inmate forgot he had this I.D. It could have been planted. He may not have known it was there. There was no picture on it yet.

When we showed it to the Captain, he wanted to know where we found it, and the inmates' name. He took it from there.

After four hours of hard work, we finished with the shakedown, and resumed our assignments, which was going to the chow hall to monitor chow lines. Chow took a very long time. Usually the entire block would go but not so today, only one half of the block went at a time, and was locked in first before more were sent. When chow was over, the officers, had to report to the control center. It was near shift change and final count.

Captain Wiggins told us about a high-speed chase, how the prisoners were caught near Glacier Lake, just 45 miles away. All three were in custody and en route to the prison as he spoke. We were told to go out to industries to check for clues that may have been overlooked by the other officers. There really wasn't time to fine-tooth comb it, so we did a routine search, and finished in time for shift change. Meanwhile, the prisoners were returned to the prison and placed directly in Ad. Seg. They were considered high risk, and would be there for quite sometime.

For the next six weeks, I was assigned with officer Rembrandt, a young man from Owendale, who relocated to Johnstown to work there. He was efficient, and direct, and to the point. Our assignment was to go into the tunnels, to check for anything out of the ordinary, and civilian workers would repair whatever was needed. We made note of what we found, and turned in our reports each day to the Captain.

The first thing I noticed when we went through the tunnels was that they were doubly secured, with heavy steel locked gates every so many feet. We furrowed our way through each tunnel; when we saw daylight, we would climb the ladder unlock the grated lid and look to see what part of the 80 acres we had arrived at. All we had to do is number each lock with the key assigned to that lock. We also had to watch for anything that could have been overlooked by the civilian maintenance workers. The job was enjoyable, and all too soon we were done inspecting the entire prison including the catwalks in each cellblock.

The escapees must have been very intelligent and dangerous. How did they get through in the first place, I asked myself? We'll never know.

They apparently confiscated a passkey, to get through the locked areas, and gates through the tunnels. Why were there tunnels under the prison? Water was piped in through pipes from the huge water tower behind the prison; also the electric wires came through pipes and the central heating plant sent steam heat through the larger pipes coming through the tunnels. All we could do was repair and make deterrents to avoid another escape.

Chapter 23

On Saturdays I usually was on the roof gun post. I relieved the day shift officer, and asked if there were any incidents during his shift. Sometimes the officer was friendly and talked, while others would say, " Read the log." Usually afternoon yard was in session when I started. When the prisoners went back to their block, and the next mass movement was industries lines getting off work. These workers got a pittance for their efforts.

Chow lines were routine, then yard. Until then my day has gone without incident.

It was during yard that I received a phone call from the Captain.

"Hello, officer Morgan? This is Captain Wiggins, I would like to ask you something."

"Yes, what is it?"

"I want you to stop wearing those flamboyant earrings."

You have to be kidding. Milk white 3/8 inch plastic earrings? Your 'girl' in the Control Center wears dangling earrings with colored rhinestones in them. Now that's flamboyant. 'Course she is African American, and beautiful, and gets favors all the time. Don't be bias; we all have to do our job.

"Sure, I'll be glad to do this for you," I said sweetly. I hesitated for a second then said, "There is something I would like if it could be possible too, Captain Wiggins."

"Yes, what is it?"

"I would like to be one of the acting Sergeants. I believe I can do it."

"This could be arranged, I'll get back with you."

"Thanks!"

This meant a $2,100 bonus after six months. I knew I could do it, was eager to prove it to myself, and anyone else who cared.

Della Daniels called me at during slow times and we talked about anything that was happening in this horrific place, as well as at home. While we were still at the academy she hinted that she might be a lesbian, or like my husband says 'left handed.' But I wasn't sure until she came right out and said it was true. She was married to a very handsome man, who gave her a beautiful little girl child they named Daniella. When the baby came he took off and left her alone to fetch for herself and the baby. It wasn't long before she moved back with her parents. They took care of little Daniella while Della worked.

She made an effort to be a good officer and a very good friend. I like her.

One night Della called me after lockdown just before the shift was over. We would have about thirty minutes to watch for anything unusual but never the less it was still a good time to unwind, talk to someone about the days incidents, a new story, or whatever.

"Dis 's DD, you're not going to believe dis. Dis prisoner came right up to me in da shack and starts up a conversation. I don' want," she stressed the 'want,' " to talk to dat honkey boy, he bein' an inmate and all. Well he say dat he was lonesome, and he watch me and see I'm a good lookin' gal from his home town."

"Well, how did he know that?" I asked.

"He's guessin', went right on sayin' dat he jus' came in from way up north in dat prison where it snows on de fourth of July, an he be lonesome. He din' know' anyone here yet."

"Look out! Remember our classes, the first set up, etc.?"

"Well, I kinda felt sorry for the poor fella."

"Come on!"

"Well, anyway I listen to him, an he in for life. You know he tol' me what he do. He done killed his wife. He misses her too."

"I'll bet he does."

"Anyways he be doin time for five year now an' he was transferred 'cause he be bangin' de librarian an' got caught. That damn fool, what he expect?"

"Right, good thing you are out in the open where he can't get to you."

"Why dat dam fool honkey thought I'd let him in my shack. You kno', I not be layin' dat way. I don' care how lonesome he be, he not getting' a part o' me."

I couldn't help but laugh. She told it like it was.

About a month later she called me again, to talk about the same topic.

"You remember dat white boy I tol' you about? Well he keep pressin' me. He say he want me in a bad way. Girl, what am I gonna' do?"

"Tell him you're not laying that way. Tell him you like women. Tell him even if you were straight that you wouldn't do what he wants, because you are a good officer and you would never even hear of jeopardizing your job over another persons needs. Tell him to get lost!"

"Well, I can't, 'cause, he be talkin' 'bout givin' me some money. Now you know I need money."

"Don't get yourself wrapped up into something you can't get away from. Your job pays more than he could offer you, besides you must know that he uses women to get what he wants. According to what you tell me he did up north."

"I guess you be right. I'll try to tell him."

"Did he ever tell you why he killed his wife?"

"No, but he owned a string of department stores in de big city."

She stopped talking about that guy not long after. She started to talk about Officer Mayberry's death. Della said they say she walked in on an orgy in the auditorium, and that's why she was killed. When I asked her how she heard about it, she said it was common knowledge that they did this all the time; this was what 'playing ball' meant.

"Dey's a click, you kno' what I mean? You be in da click you play ball, an' you don' have de bad assignments. Dey be takin' the good lookin' black girls wif' de big shots too; white girls too, along wif' de o'cers and do as dey please, 'cause dey wan' a good assignment, an' dey like it too, I guess."

I whistled under my breath.

"That's pretty heavy, do you believe this with all your heart?"

"Why not? It figures. No prisoner is goin' to kill her when you know as well as I that he could't possibly get in dere or even want to when everythin' he need be in de kitchen."

I stored this in my mind to add to my journal, when I got home. It was possible. I remembered what the porter told me and the two other stories corresponded.

"What about your 'boy' has he finally given up. You haven't mentioned him for awhile?"

"Well, he be still pressin, but now he wan' me to get some money."

"What? How does he expect you to do that?" I asked.

"He jus' say for me to go to de lawyer, an ask him to get it for him, den when he give it to me, I bring it in."

"How do you expect to bring it in? How much does he want? This is dangerous. I wouldn't do it. You'll get caught, and boom you are out a job," I said.

She wasn't listening to me; I shook my head as she continued.

"Well he say he wan' $25,000. Dat be quite a bit to put up my 'gina. An' dat's de other thin' he be sayin' dat he be in love with me. He be talkin' to me for almost six month, I don' really know what to believe."

"Oh, Della, I am concerned. I hope you will not do anything to jeopardize your position, or bring harm to your family. He is here because he has done an injustice to the community, broken the laws of our land and our Lord in Heaven. Killing is one of the Ten

Commandments. I can't stress my feelings strongly enough. I consider you to be a good officer and most of all a good friend. Please understand." I pled with her.

"I do, or I wouldn't talk to you 'bout dis, and I am thinkin'," she said and we said 'good-bye.'

Two weeks later she called again.

"I be in deep trouble. Anne, what am I gonna do? I brought in $2,500 to him. He got it and was happy. Now he mad an' say he gonna get me, he gonna get my little girl, 'cause he claim de attorney gave me 25,000. Dat's a lie, he didn't."

"Why would he say that unless it was the truth?"

"Well, maybe de lawyer keep it," She said.

"Della, tell me the truth, what actually happened?"

"Well, I go see da lawyer, we go to de bank, he get the money, all of it. Den he give me extra' cause he say Ronald wan' me to have some. I try to put it in a tight roll and put it you know where, an' it wouldn't fit. So I keep makin'' it smaller, and decide to keep the rest and jus' give him the 2,500. How would he know how much de lawyer gave me?"

"Oh Lord, woman, it's a small world here, you are in trouble, God help you."

"I gonna tell Godfry in 'I & I' 'bout it, den maybe I can get outta dis. My Mother took my little Daniella to Mississippi to visit my aunt there."

"Good Luck. Keep in touch, and let me know what happens."

That was the last time I talked to her.

Gossip said she took a leave. I read the Headlines of the newspaper, " Mr. William Daniels, killed in drive-by shooting." William Daniels was Della's father.

Chapter 24

Idleman was sitting behind his desk when Sam came through the door without knocking.

"What's the meaning of you're not paying Mayberry the $250,000.00? Just three weeks ago I directly told you that it was a go, and to cut a check for him."

"There's a miscommunication here. I wasn't finished investigating him."

"You! You weren't finished investigating him? Who are you, Idleman? What makes you, a weasel of a man, think that your decision is final?" Sam shouted.

"But he may have done her in to get the inheritance."

"Enough, enough about that cock and bull story. His wife was killed while she was on duty; he and his daughter have suffered enough. They have waited for three years for this check."

"Yes sir, I know but…"

"No buts, cut that check immediately, or I'll have your job so fast it will make your head swim."

"Yes sir, yes sir, Mary, cut the check for Mr. Mayberry."

Mary smiled pleasantly and proceeded to cut the check.

Chapter 25

The night was hot and sticky. The red of the sunset faded into darkness. All prison major traffic was over; the prisoners were roaming freeing their block just before night lock-down and final count.

This was partially normal. For the most part the residents were locked in already; some were straggling from their shower, and some were block reps, or porters. They usually would slide into their cell just before the top-locks were slammed into place.

"Shoot the S.O.B.! Shoot!" blasted through the radios.

"Man down on Base. Officer down on base!"

Big Red went off.

"Someone call an ambulance! Officer Lowery has been hit!"

"Control center to 'A"Block, an ambulance is on it's way."

The yard crew reached the block before the bang of big red went off. The desk officer was stabbed with a shank, right in front of the Sgt. and a base officer. He was loosing blood fast, one of the officers held the shank steady to slow the bleeding.

The ambulance crew lowered Lowery onto the gurney and rolled him into the ambulance. It would take a very good surgeon to save his life.

The officers, who saw the incident go down, were stunned. Officers in the block and other assignments, who heard it on the radios couldn't believe Lowery was stabbed either. It would take a very good surgeon to save his life. Some prayed, while other officers were cussing.

The Captain called for total lock-down immediately. Shift change was upon the prison, so the shift would go home and the day shift would have a total shakedown.

Lowery was one of the best officers. He went by the book. He was known as a Christian, a good family man, and always went home on time. Never even swore.

Approximately 27 officers went over to the hospital after work, to wait and see how Lowery was doing. He was still in surgery. We all waited in the waiting room. Some were talking about how it happened. Others were swearing to get the prisoner when they could.

"All he was doing when it happened, was setting up the schedule for the day shift, when bam, he got it." Said Riley, the base officer.

"Told Greenville, the officer with him almost lost his false teeth when he yelled 'shoot the bastard'." Officer Maynard from second gallery said.

"Yah, I was on the roof when I heard him on the radio, I couldn't tell what was happening." Officer Coupling said.

"When I heard Big Red go off, I nearly jumped out of my shoes," one of the female officers on first gallery said. "It was so loud that all I could think was we were being bombed."

"I looked down from my gallery, through the smoke from the shot gun to see what was happening, and saw the prisoner running away from the desk. Then two officers tackled him and took him out of the block," Julia Brown said.

"I shot Big Red off, I should have shot the prisoner," Said officer Nagel. He was obviously shaken.

"No, he will get what's coming," Lieutenant Jones said.

"Wait and see, we won't forget too soon," Said Nagel.

"Wonder why anyone would want to hurt Lowery?" asked officer Peasley.

"That's right, Lowery is a model officer," The lieutenant added.

"We'll just have to hope and pray that he comes out of this," I said.

Many hung their heads while others did all the talking. We all were hoping for the best, and waiting.

Finally the doctor came out of surgery. He looked surprised to see so many of us there waiting to hear the news.

"He's going to be fine. The shank didn't hit any vital organs. With surgery complete it will just be the healing process. He will be here for a few days, though. You can keep praying for him if you wish," Dr. Blankenhorn said.

Some of the guys smirked, others looked like, 'Yah that was a good idea.'

Slowly, a few at a time left the waiting room and went home.

The following work shift we were told that the 233 rifles would be replaced with a mini fourteen, semi-automatic rifle. The clip held ten shells and when you fired a shot, the next shell automatically went into the chamber.

We had to re-qualify with the new rifles. A few at a time went to the gun range across the street during our shift to acquaint our selves with the new rifle.

We were taught the rifle check procedure for the mini-14; Safety – "ON' position, remove magazine from weapon, lock bolt to the rear visually and manually, then check the chamber, check barrel for obstructions, inspect the overall condition of the weapon, pull back on bolt and let it return home, forward position, insert magazine back in weapon, make sure safety is "On" position.

We were told that at no time should our fingers be on the trigger guard or onto the trigger of the rifle, except to fire.

At the shooting range we each shot separately, using three targets to qualify.

At least two targets had to be 75 points or better to qualify. The recoil was a little different, but it was easy for me to shoot and still get straight in the center of the target. I qualified with the first two targets.

The range Sgt. said, "Go back inside, you are good to go."

My buddy Frank said, "Dummy, now you have to go back earlier than us."

I didn't care. I was pleased with myself. Three years ago shooting was the last thing I thought I'd ever do, and there I was shooting and doing a good job of it.

One day soon after that I did have the opportunity to really shoot.

Chow lines were in session, 'A' and 'B' blocks were done, and the first half of 'C' Block was leaving the dining room exit to go back to the other side of the prison. Soon after leaving, a group of inmates surrounded a weaker prisoner and were pushing him back and forth. They started to close in on him. I knew the little prisoner was going to be stuck; I knew it just by their actions.

I quickly looked to see if the other roof officer was anywhere to cover this altercation: nowhere.

I shot a warning shot in the ground about twenty feet away from the crowd. The prisoners broke up immediately. Officers ran out from the chow hall, cuffed the little one and took him to protective custody. The predators scrambled as soon as they heard the rifle go off.

Within minutes, I got a phone call, asking me why I shot. It was the Captain, I calmly told him why, " I could not see an officer nearer to the altercation."

I thought of my instructor at the academy, 'many things will happen in there, and you, only you will be the one to make a 'judgment call', and follow through.'

"Thank you," the captain said, "Please write a memo, saying just what you said to me."

"Yes, sir, I will do that right away." I answered.

Later I found out another officer shot simultaneously with me from the other side of his post shack, out of my vision. Only one shot was heard, yet the ground crew saw both bullets hit the ground. We both were asked to submit memo's to document our actions for the Governor.

Both Roberts and my 'judgment calls' were warranted, and we were not reprimanded for our actions.

Lowery healed fast and soon he was back to work. By the time he returned, many had heard from the prisoners why he was 'stuck.'

"He be too rigid with his rules."

"He don' bend one inch."

"We be warning him. He don' listen."

"He be makin' my 'homie' mad an' he done got him."

"We have our ways, you'se have yours."

"I tried to tell him, but he didn't believe me."

A short time later I was working the post where Big Red is shot from, when my partner called me over to see something going on in fourth gallery. When I looked out my peek hole towards the gallery two inmates were standing on opposite sides of the bars. The big one – a porter - had his penis out, and the inmate in the cell began to perform oral sex. I couldn't write him up unless he had eye-to-eye contact with me, so I hit the steel wall to attract his attention. The porter knew then he was in trouble; he shook his fist and called me a 'honkey white bitch.' My partner, officer Schenigal, said to write him up. Schinegal knew this Porters name and cell number so I wrote him up.

The next day I was called to the control center. The Lieutenant on staff that day wanted to review the ticket I wrote.

She started reading it, "On Oct. 23, 1990 while working in the gun turret between 'A' and 'B' Blocks I directly observed Porter James Cunningham insert his throbbing member into the mouth of locked in prisoner, Tom Miller, at cell number 4, which was approximately…Ha Ha Ha. You can't write 'throbbing member,' how do you know it was throbbing?"

"It was bobbing up and down." I said looking down at my feet.

"Ha ha haha ha ha, I don't believe you wrote this." She couldn't hold back her laughing.

"What do you want it to say, I'll change it?" I asked.

"Okay, and did your partner see this incident too?" the Lieutenant asked.

"Yes, he saw it first and told me to write him up, that he would witness it."

"Alright, I'll call him down later. Thanks. Have a seat and re-write it right now so I can take it to the counselor to have it reviewed. You know the porter will lose his job. But that's his problem, he knew better."

I sat down at her desk, rewrote the ticket, and then handed it to her. She read it and said it looked good and that it should fly.

"Girl, you are a trip. You sure made me laugh," she said as I turned to leave.

The Captain came out of his office and called to me, "Officer Morgan, come in here a minute."

"Yes, sir," I said as I walked into his office.

"Have a seat. Do you still want to be temporary Sergeant?"

"Yes, I do."

"Good, you will start next week. Your pay will remain the same, your days off will be Monday and Tuesday, and we need you for the weekend. When six months are over you will receive a bonus check for $2,100 or something around that amount. Maybe a little more, give or take."

"Thanks!"

I walked out of the control center offices with a little lighter step that I didn't have for quite some time.

It was remarkable how fast those six months went by. Everything went well, most of the officers gave me the best support possible. Each assignment worked out smoothly, with very little incidents.

Although one incident stayed in my memory, it was the day I covered for the Sgt. in 'B' Block. I was sitting at the desk, in a glassed-in office, when I heard a scurrying of feet outside. Some officers were running towards the north end of base. I ran out just in time to see a prisoner fall five levels, from the fourth gallery to base. It was Bruno Jackson, his head was crushed, but he was still alive. Blood was coming from his eyes and ears. I called the prison Hospital for the mini ambulance. The yard crew came rushing in and the gate officers watched for the ambulance. I ordered the block officers to lock down all galleries, and all prisoners to return to their cells.

The prisoner was moaning, and rolling his eyes. I leaned over him and asked what happened.

"Pressing me, two of them," he grunted out

"What are their names, the ones that were pressing you?" I asked.

"Mojo, an' Slippery," he said softly.

"Okay, just relax, the ambulance is almost here."

Mojo was the big Puerto Rican, porter for fourth gallery. I wasn't sure who 'Slippery' is. I'd have to get with the officers later to get the story straight before writing my report.

It took six minutes totally for the ambulance to arrive. Bruno was barely breathing. I was sure he wouldn't last long enough to get to the hospital.

With the block locked in, I took time to confer with my officers. Each would write a memo to say what they saw. The two officers from the fourth gallery witnessed most of it and tickets were issued to the two prisoners who were responsible.

I checked with the two officers in the gun post, to see if they saw what happened, since it was closer to them than us down on base. I had them write memos too. I talked with the Roof Sgt. and the Yard Sgt. they also would put in reports, or have the officers that were a part of this incident, write reports. Then I wrote my report to the Captain.

Another incident was similar.

"Sergeant, you have to help me," a prisoner said reaching for my arm.. His eyes looked pleadingly sad.

"What's the problem?" I asked.

"I lent my radio to my homie and he won't give it back."

"Who is your homie?" I asked.

"He lives on my gallery, and he said I gave it to him."

"Who is your homie, where does he lock?"

"On third gallery, cell number 27."

"I'll see what I can do."

I called the counselor and relayed the story to him.

"Do you know what he is in here for?" He asked me.

"No, I don't. Tell me." I said.

"He murdered his wife, chopped her up, and fed her to his dog."

"Why?"

"She knew he was raping his boy scouts, and threatened to tell."

I had read about the raping in the paper.

Twin brothers turned him in, by telling their mother. Later, others confessed that he had molested them too.

"Shit! What a creep," I said.

"And that's why he has nothing coming. He gets what he gets. I'll take care of it."

"Okay, thanks."

They look innocent until you find out what they did and what they are in for.

Chapter 26

"Hello, this is Max Idleman, how can I help you?"

"Hello, this is Don Mayberry, I'm wondering when I will get my check for the insurance settlement?"

"You will have to refresh me," Idleman stalled. "Which settlement was this?"

"You know very well Idleman, this has gone for three-and-a half years. I have debts. I'm going to lose my house and all I have invested in."

"Oh, yes, you are the husband who works one day a week and purchased a $180,000 home with the understanding that you will get $250,000 from the state in the death of your wife."

"Yes, and they put the culprit who killed her in for three lifetimes up north in snow country. Shouldn't that be enough to convince you I had nothing to do with it."

"Well, as a matter-of-fact, I investigated the possibility you may have hired him to kill her. If you remember a few years back, a prisoner was let out to kill a senator and then brought back. He lived in the best of luxury possible, although he was still locked in for the rest of his natural life."

"Don't go there my friend, because I can get you for slander. Do I have to go over your head to the district manager?"

"No, no, no, you'll be hearing from me before the week ends." He had the check for a few months, but waited to hear from Mayberry.

"That sounds more like it. "Mayberry said.

True to his word Mr. Don Mayberry received his check by Friday, the same week.

He also received the inheritance from his first wife's family, and moved to Illinois where his little girl had lived with her grandfather. He gave up the home he tried to purchase; it was long gone after the long wait for the check. He paid rent until he couldn't any longer. The owner was patient and would have applied the rent as part of the purchase. When the big inheritance came in, he took his old Ford and migrated west to the home he knew in his younger years, to reacquaint himself to the daughter that he hardly knew.

When Mayberry told Diane this, and that he was leaving state and going out to the mid-west to live with his daughter, she called to tell me.

"Hi, this is Anne," I said.

"I'm calling to tell you the latest about Mayberry," Diane said.

"What about him?'

"The check finally came in the mail, and he is moving out west to be with his daughter. He also received the inheritance from the prior marriage. Since he was single when the old man died ... you know that was the clause for him to receive it," she said.

"No, I didn't know that," I said. "I'm happy for him."

"Yah, me too."

"How have you been?" I asked.

"Okay, I'm still going to the counselor, trying to get my act together. Still meeting with the girls monthly."

"Sounds good, if you hear anything you think I need to hear please call me. We'll get together soon, and do keep in touch," I said.

"All right, later." Diane said.

DW Susan Lorenzo was trying to get hold of me. She left messages on my phone. I really didn't have anything substantial to talk to her about. I could have told her about the officer that was definitely dirty, or I could have told her about the officer in 'D' Block who was a little too close to the inmates, and even acted like one himself, but she told me to watch the only one that I didn't have a report to give.

However, during one time while I was acting Sgt. in 'A' Block, officer Julia Brown worked on second gallery. It was easy to see her moves from the Sgt. desk. I didn't want to be obvious, but when she stayed at a certain cell for more than a few brief moments, I could look up the inmate, in the files. The one inmate, in particular, was the same one she made contact with on the yard eight months prior, Nathaniel Johnson. He was in for selling dope.

Johnson was the inmate to watch; who he contacted, what his activities were, and how often officer Brown spent any length of time with him. Also, when she made an excuse to leave the block. It was necessary to follow her, and see if she met the honey-colored skinned prisoner on the south yard again. That blue-eyed beauty lived in 'C' Block. I saw him in the visiting room one day when I had front gate duty. His wife was a beauty too, dressed to the nines from head to toe. They appeared to have money. I never asked what he was in for. I saw him in the prison barber shop; he had an expensive finger wave hair do. Usually paid with favors.

I knew it was time I called her, so I and dialed her number.

"Hi, Susan, this is Anne."

"I was wondering when you were going to make contact," Susan replied.

"I received your message that you left on the answer machine."

"That was the third one, I began to wonder if you had changed your mind. You could have called back, my husband is out of the country again; he does those triathlon events all over the world."

"No, I didn't change my mind. I really didn't have anything on her yet, that is, to take time to contact you."

"Listen, anything is important. Tell me what you know so far."

I related all that I had seen so far. I added that I don't think she could do much with what I learned. I told her about the time that officer Brown had walked right through the checkpoint gate and went into

'D' block, where she stayed for about ten minutes, then returned back the way she came.

"Hum. This is interesting. I'll get someone on that. I'm glad you didn't mention any names, because you never know when your phone is tapped."

"Oops, I didn't think about that," I said apologetically.

"Yes, so the next time when you call back, just say when you and I can have lunch. Okay?"

"Got it." I said.

I still wondered how she gets the dope, if she is dirty. Also how is she able to spread it to those who are her connections? This was what Susan needed. Susan's' concerns are dope traffic in the prison. She as good as said this. FBI being involved would make it dope, smuggling over the border.

Chapter 27

A new officer came in about six months ago, just before I was made acting sergeant. He is very tall and attractive with a military look; clean cut, polite, and professional. Officer Wilson would stop to talk to me on his way to the bathroom. What I first noticed about him was he had a way of asking questions that were personal, but not fresh. He was being friendly in a way that was easy to talk to.

He asked me where I lived, why I was working here, and if I like it. It made me feel free to ask the same questions in return.

He lived in town in an old home that probably belonged to one of the early founders of Johnstown. It had an Italian design, and a huge marble fireplace. He described it so well that I had a visual picture immediately. The area it was in, however, started to go downhill. He said he believes there is dope trafficking in the area and wants to move to a better part of town. He is married, with two children, a boy and a girl. His wife worked for the government. They moved there from a Davenport, about fifty miles east of Johnstown.

He is one of the twelve. I'm sure of it. I knew he couldn't say for a fact, nor could I, or the other ten. I don't know if I really wanted to know who the prisoners were. As often as they were transferred in and out, it would be easy to do without any of the administration in the way. I still wonder what the purpose of it is, in the long run. What does the government want with the situations here in the prison? Do they want to take over the state property and turn them into federal prisons? I overheard someone say hat once in roll -call. Do they think if the Feds have control, they can find the drug lords on a bigger scale? The warden quoted to the local paper that drugs were more prevalent now, more than ever, causing murders among the inmates. The Feds could possibly know contacts following from the little man to the top. All I know is that I was to watch certain people, report it, and wait for more orders. Why was I doing this? Was it because I looked up to the DW? Was it because I was the very best officer, doing my very best, and knowing that I did do the very best?

I continued doing my job, keeping quiet, and watching. I was always watching.

I was working, as a spare in the chow hall when Sgt. Wharton called me to his podium. He stood there during chow lines. He said I was wanted in the control center.

On my way to the control center Captain Wiggins met me half way across the marble floor of the big room.

"We have a problem. Officer Kuhn, and Officer Selby went to the prison hospital to get a prisoner from Ad. Seg., who was treated for his oozing sores. Now, the old coot, half crazy and with the disease that he has, refuses to return back to Ad. Seg. unless 'Agent 99' comes to get him. They have been trying for two hours to convince him to return to his lock. You are, 'Agent 99' until he is back in his cell. All you have to do is go to the hospital and say that 'Agent 99' has arrived to take him back."

I just looked at him for a second. I wanted to laugh it was so strange. "Yes sir, I can do that."

"I wouldn't ask you if I didn't think you could do it."

He always had a gruff way about himself. I never knew how to take him.

"Thank you, Captain, I appreciate that."

I only knew he had a disease that had to be treated; what it was I did not know. He had to be a little off to request 'Agent99.' He was what we called a 'bug'. He was smarter than the average bear, if he could get away with this stunt.

I reached the door at the south end of the hospital. The officers in charge of the door saw me coming and pressed the buzzer to let me in.

Officer Kuntz was pacing back and forth like a tiger in a cage, I thought I saw smoke rolling out of his ears. He definitely was livid over the situation. Of course, how would it look to not be able to get a prisoner to return to his lock until 'Agent 99' arrived to escort him back, and the Agent turns out to be a woman!

He rushed me and said, "Okay this is what has happened. He had his treatment, and refused to leave. Would not take one step until you arrived."

"Okay, let's do it. Where is he?" I asked.

"In the waiting room with Officer Selby. Selby is easygoing, so I left him with the 'bug,' I knew I would blow if I stayed in there too long. I've been watching through the windows."

I looked up and saw that the waiting room was half wooden walls and half windows. At any given time, or angle, the room was great for officers to observe the prison patients through the glass.

I walked in, followed by O. Kuhn, "Officer Selby I'm agent 99 reporting for duty, sir. To take Mr. Beacomb back to his 'house.'"

Prisoner Beacomb went to open his mouth to say something, when O. Kuhn grabbed him by the arm and said, "Let's go!"

Selby and Kuhn helped Beacomb to his feet, swung him around and headed to the door. Beacomb was silent for the first hundred yards, and then he found his voice and said, "Are you Agent 99?"

"Yes I am," I answered.

Beacomb went on to say, "I appreciate your dropping everything with your busy schedule to come all this way from headquarters to escort me back to my 'house.'"

"Oh, that's all right."

Kuhn lowered his face to my level and said under his breath, "Don't feed him, I have heard from him enough for one day." The words came through a locked jaw, teeth clamped shut while his two hands clenched into fists. He was livid.

"Oops, okay."

We were turning the corner almost back to the gate opening to Ad. Seg., when Beacomb said, "Now, I'm going with Agent 99 right straight through the check point gate, through control center, and right out the front gate, right '99'?"

Kuhn grabbed him and said, "You're going right here!" Selby had the gate open, and Beacomb was rushed through with the help of both officers. Kuhn and Selby went in to take the ankle chains off; when I saw Beacomb's legs. There were oozing open sores all over his legs. Selby released the handcuffs and Kuhn pushed him on his bunk rather roughly. The door was slammed shut, and I breathed a sigh of relief. The deed was done.

Now I could go back to just plain officer Morgan. I finished my assignment in the control center, and went home.

Driving home, I thought about how Kuntz acted; a little rough, and definitely upset. He normally worked on a gun post was not a good candidate for close contact with prisoners. I put this in my journal when I arrived home, along with the other events of the day.

Logging this days events were slightly humorous, yet I often added the days' events anyway.

I thought about the Mayberry killing; at the trial it was proven that there was blood on Willie the kitchen worker's shirt, and in his cell. It was supposed to prove that Willie Robinson was the killer. How did he get from the south side over to the north side, kill her and return with blood all over his shirt? How did he get back through the gate to the south side, passing all sorts of witness, with nobody stopping him?

This is what I believe; the plot to kill her took just a moment. She walked in on something she should not have seen. Knowing that she wouldn't 'play ball,' they had to shut her up. She screamed, so he pulled his belt off and tightened it around her neck to shut her up. One of them raped her, the one with blond hair. It wasn't Willie who killed her, he is black, his pubic hair is black. It was a fact that a blond pubic hair was found on her, but it was lost. Mayberry claimed that there was more than one type of semen found in her vagina also.

Poor Willie Robinson was a victim of circumstance, and a man who was willing to take the rap, after he was promised a better life in the mountains in 'snow country.' He would live like a rich man, and never have a worry again. He already had life without parole. What more could he get for a murder that he didn't commit?

I think the shirt was taken from Willie's cell, wiped in the blood, and planted back in Willies cell, when it would be discovered later.

Two officers involved, in one way or another, quit their jobs and left the state. Another stayed and put on a very good act. Some of the administration transferred out. One put a bullet in his head. One woman involved was promoted to Secretary to the warden.

All this was scuttlebutt. What was the truth? Only time will reveal the truth.

What if Willie did kill her? She should have been smart enough to ask questions, when Willie asked her to let him in for supplies. She would have asked him why he didn't have what he needed in the kitchen.

Willie would not have taken his bloody shirt to his lock. If he did, he wanted to be caught. But why would he want to be caught? Was someone pressing him for sex, drugs, or money? Did he want to be transferred to another prison, for his safety? Trouble would only follow him.

O. Mayberry was found with her keys, in the parking lot. The bloody radio that was at the crime scene was not hers. The belt that was around her neck couldn't have been Willie's. He was poor, and only had state supplied clothing, and shoes, belt, etc.

A porter had told me that 'it be de o'cers' who done it. I was told he was transferred out to a medium security prison. Had someone heard him telling me about her walking in on the orgy?

Chapter 28

The answer machine was blinking when I came in from mowing my lawn. The message said, "Call me when you get in, it's the Captain."

Now what?

"Hello, Captain Wiggins please," I said.

"Who is calling?" the female voice asked.

"Officer Morgan." I said.

"Hi! I want you to know your request to be transferred to housing has been accepted. You will start Tuesday, in 'A' Block on the west side. Report to Sgt. Rogers, he is already informed that you will be coming. You realize you will get a pay hike? Hope this is what you want. You know once you transferred to housing; it will take an act of congress to get back out. Good Luck. See you in here. Oh, your days off will be Sunday and Monday." Said Captain Wiggins.

"Okay, thanks. See you Tuesday."

This move will be great; I can go to Church again being off on Sunday. Susan Lorenzo must have had something to do with my promotion; she probably figures I can watch the Julia Brown better.

Sunday afternoon my phone rang, "Hello?"

"Hello, this is Susan, we need to have lunch. When do you have a day off, so we can meet?"

"You mean you really do not know that I have tomorrow off?" I asked her.

"No, why?"

"We can meet tomorrow, Monday at the same restaurant, House of Chin, okay? Or did you have something else in mind?" I said.

"No, that will be fine." She said.

"Around one o'clock alright?"

"Sure," Susan said.

"See you then."

I spent the remaining part of Sunday relaxing. Since my second day off would be split in two, I could catch up with the laundry in the morning, meet Susan for lunch, and still have the evening to relax.

It was precisely two minutes before 1p.m. when I drove into the parking lot of House of Chin Restaurant. I looked across the parking lot at the Mercedes and realized that Susan was already there. I parked my Dodge pickup and walked into the restaurant.

Susan was sitting at a booth on my left, in the sunshine. I slipped into the shaded side, which suited me because I could see her eyes better, and scrutinize her every move.

"Hi, Susan, you look nice today." She was wearing a floor length skirt, with a navy colored blazer to match. The lace trimmed off white blouse added to and complimented her outfit and auburn red hair. "Are you coming from work?"

"Yes," she said, "I worked for four hours and decided to take the rest of the day off."

"Shall we order?"

"I have already, for you and me. Hot tea is okay isn't it?" Susan asked.

"Sure, surprise me. I like surprises."

"Well here's another surprise. You will not have to watch officer. Brown anymore, I have taken care of that situation."

"Oh. No questions, right?"

"Right. But I want you to watch someone else. He is a prisoner. He seems to be all over the prison, goes where he pleases. I want to know why. I want to know where he goes, what he does, and who he talks to. You will be assigned to his block, also the block that officer Brown works. Leave her alone, but if you see something that is more than the ordinary, let me know." Susan said.

"Okay, I will do just that. The prisoner, who is he? Why are you particularly interested in him?" I asked her.

"His name is Alexander Bartholomew, he likes to be called Alex. He lives on second gallery. I'm trying to decide if he is one of 'us.'"

"You mean one of the 12? I thought you knew who they were." I said.

"Yes, he's one of the twelve, but I think he is dirty. I need to know. And, no, I don't know everything." Susan said.

"I'll do what I can." I said. "You know I will be acting sgt. beginning tomorrow's shift?"

"No, I didn't, this will be good, but will it hinder your assignment with me?"

"I'm hoping it won't, I'll do my best though."

Our food was delivered just as we finish talking. We forgot our talk and enjoyed the beef and broccoli over fried rice. We made small talk for the remaining part of lunch. At about three o'clock we both walked out of House of Chin to leave to our respective homes.

I began to doubt the DW. It would be an assumption to say that she was truly working with the FBI. It would also be an assumption to say that there were 12 agents in the same prison. What would possibly be the reason to have that many watching and for what? Anything out of the ordinary, she said.

My new subject, Alex, was indeed all over. He had access to many parts of the prison, …that was out of the ordinary.

"She go all places, an' odd times, she be seein' a prisoner," I recalled D.D. saying to me one day. She was talking about Peggy. When I asked her how she knew, she answered, that a prisoner told me. Once

Peggy was assigned to a civilian plumber and his crew of prisoners. It gave her ample time to go to 'the restroom', take a lunch break, return when she pleased.

One day D.D. saw her go through the cross- corridor gates using her passkey, to enter the hallway to the 'restroom', but she walked past the restroom, and through another gate, where she disappeared. Twenty minutes later she came from where she disappeared, walking towards D.D., looking suspicious. Her hair was all mussed up, shirt was half sticking out of her belted slacks, and the back of the shirt being noticeably dirty, which wasn't the case before she disappeared. The prisoner who was with her stood at the gate on the farther end of the hall, looking through the barred gate waiting to see her disappear out to the North yard. There she would return to escorting the civilian plumber and his prisoner crew.

D.D. described the prisoner to me. He was the light skinned, light blue-eyed inmate that officer Brown contacted in the South Yard.

This information was never reported to the DW. She didn't ask me to watch Peggy. Peggy was on her own, if she was dirty, God help her. I wonder what her husband would think about her actions?

Watch him and the others that were acting questionable. Why? There was more than one questionable character that needed watching. For my own knowledge, and my journal.

Too bad D.D. was no longer working for the D.O.C. She came up with a lot of good information. It certainly would be impossible to be everywhere at the same time. I felt that I couldn't trust anyone as much as I trusted her. We were true friends.

Genevive was in her own world. She worked like a robot; meticulously doing just what she was instructed, and nothing more. She could only focus on one thing at a time. When she left to go home she was a different person, and never mentioned what went on in there. She liked to relax, and did whatever it took to do just that. I respected her private life, but it was not the same as mine.

One night after work, she bumped me as we were leaving, and asked me to meet her at the Runway Bar near the airport.

When I arrived she called me over to a truck, not hers, and invited me into the passenger side. I was introduced to her friend Duke, and she wanted me to try cocaine by sucking it off a spoon into my mouth.

"This stuff is expensive, isn't it?" I asked, stalling her.

"Ya, but just suck it in. You'll like it," She said.

So I sucked it in while she continued saying that it was worth at least $20 for the amount that was in the tiny spoon.

"I don't feel anything, what is supposed to happen?" I asked.

I lied, it did relax me, but I didn't want to admit it. I wanted to be in control at all times.

"It'll mellow you out, and help you forget what happens 'in there.'"

I was disappointed in her attitude, she went on to say she used it after work often, and her 'friend' wanted me to get into it too. Well I didn't feel anything. I don't even like to get drunk, I like to be in control. Genevive and I drifted apart after that.

Diane was too wrapped up in her husband and children. She had some bad experiences that seemed to stick with her; so she was not a good confidant, which I really needed.

Ralph had taken off again. This time it was on a new assignment out of the country.

I was on my own.

Chapter 29

The local newspaper interviewed the warden, remembering the eighties; he talked about the riots that took place about eight years before. He went on to say that there is increased gang activity inside the prison because inmates are seeking illegal drugs. Just like on the streets, prisoners want the hard stuff.

And he's just the guy who knows just exactly what is going on. The first time I suspected him was that night when he personally met the truck with the chicken at the rear dock of the prison.

Warden Hale went on to say that there always were gangs before, but they weren't into the drugs like they are now. They will kill now; before, that was rare.

He was already planting seeds to cover his tracks. Of course that's only my rendition of what I believe is happening. I was still guessing. I need more information.

He changed the subject to the fact that 205 officers were hired that year, and 200 transferred out. The turnover in personnel is high, although many were transferring to another prison he stated.

The State Police and the FBI began investigating alleged corruption in the prison. The investigation was on going at that time. The warden blamed the increased violence on the overcrowding in the prisons and said he believes there should be a program to get to the youngsters before they came into the prison system, after that it would be hard to turn them around.

He certainly looked good on paper. Why do I mistrust him so vehemently? All I know is that he spends a lot of time with Alex, and like we were taught it's for money, sex, or drugs. Which of the three was it?

The message on Bob North's answering machine said to call the warden, Mike Hale.

He dialed his number. The one he gave him proved to be his home phone.

"Hello?" Mike answered.

"North, here."

"Yes, you have been waiting for my call, today I want to meet you in the parking lot at the prison. This is a better place than here or my office," the warden said.

"What time?"

"As soon as you can get there, I'm on my ay right now."

North piloted for many jobs. He was sure Mike wanted him for a flight. He flew for the governor of Arkansas hauling guns to the Contras, and bringing in cocaine in return. He was never caught. The news never knew, or if the media did know it was quieted, and never released.

North was slick, quiet, and even secretive. He told very little of his private life. No one was the wiser if he did anything unlawful. He was slick like Teflon, nothing stuck to him.

He turned into the parking lot and noticed Mike Hales Mercedes parked against the fence, away from other parked cars. North drove up beside him. Locked his door as he slid into the passenger side of Hales' car.

"Okay, what do you want to talk about?" North asked.

"North, my man, I have a flight for you to take. Can you get a trustworthy plane that will fly to Columbia and back without any breakdowns?" Hale asked.

"It will take a couple days, but yes, I can."

"What I need is for you to be able to fly below the radar, in some areas, so you won't be detected. You know how long it will take, and how much fuel you will need. I will tell you what, where and when as soon as I know. When I do know, I will expect you to keep in touch with me and be precise on the time you will land, so my contact will be there to pick up your cargo. You may have a passenger from time to time. Don't ask questions. Just do as you are told."

"Err…….okay, I'll get right on it," North said.

"Call me as soon as you are ready."

Chapter 30

My first day in the block was different. I spent two weeks while doing on-the-job-training, but this was real. In the two weeks training, I wrote a ticket when a prisoner reached out between the bars in front of me as I approached his cell. In the ticket I called it assault, and it flew. The residents knew I was fair but firm. The prisoners needed to know how I would run my gallery. I expected the cells to be clean. When I shook down a cell and found dope, I would flush it down the toilet. If I found it the second time, there would be a ticket. If I found 'spud juice,' alcoholic drink made from potatoes, it was a ticket. If I found a shank, the prisoner is automatically escorted to Ad. Seg., he was done with general population

It didn't take very long before things were going pretty good. During a routine shake down, I found approximately 29 bottles of spud juice, (home made alcohol), it was in the Block Porter's cell. Roy Farrington had some freedom to go to other cells and talk to them about what's up. He really wasn't allowed to do this, so I wrote him a ticket. After the ticket he was irate. This was his income, he said. I told him it was against the law. The result of the ticket was 'loss of privileges,' and his job.

Another inmate on my gallery was young, attractive, Albanian, in for 15 years for selling narcotics on the street. He called me to his cell one day shortly after I started in the block, when I reached it; he was standing there naked and smiling. I kept going and let him suffer for not getting a reaction from me. I didn't write a ticket.

I waited a few days to shake down his cell. I found some marijuana and flushed it down the toilet. I heard a shout from down the gallery, "You white honkey bitch!"

"Crime doesn't pay," I called back sarcastically.

Mandy, my new subject doesn't live on my gallery, he is on the gallery below me and just as the DW said, he was everywhere. When he was in the block he would pop up from any one of the galleries, talking with this inmate and that inmate. He always carried a clipboard, looking somewhat official. Finally one day he approached me.

"Why did you have to throw out the porter's spud juice anyway?" he said.

"It stunk, I wouldn't have found it otherwise. And it is procedure to do just that, after the evidence is proven."

"Well, why did you flush my man's pot?"

"I warned him and all of my gallery that this was what I would do if I found anything of that category."

He shook his head back and forth, "Well I guess that was fair enough, but why didn't you write him up?"

"If I find it again, I will. I promised that too."

"Well, you're some.." he started to say.

"Officer," I interjected.

I think I just broke the ice with this guy, I thought, *as he sauntered off the gallery.*

Someone cat called at him, and he said, "Thanks". He had an average build, about 5 feet 11 inches, brown eyes and dark hair streaked with silver. He had been around for a while.

I was standing in the dining room of the Mess Hall and I noticed one of the officers, Dan Romley, peering out of the window between the officer dining room and prisoner chow hall. He was looking directly at Alex. As usual, Alex was being quite the social butterfly.

"Hi, Dan, what are you looking at so intently?"

"Ah, this guy gets me here," he tapped his tummy. "You know, gut feelings." He was referring to Alex.

"Hum, have you seen him around much?"

This is a great opportunity for me to find out something about Alex. I figured Dan would know more than I wished to hear. He grunted, and hesitated before he finally started his narration.

"He was in protective custody," Dan said. " I was in the gun turret. I saw him go in a cell, but I didn't know there was another prisoner in there already. Not until the gallery officer stopped and said ' What's going on in there?' The next thing I know the officer started to open the cell, then hesitated. I jumped to a larger peek hole, and stuck my rifle out the hole, sat it back down and grabbed 'Big Red', the officer looked up and came my way. 'Hey, he hollered at me, I'm going down for back up." Then I yelled, 'stay there, I'll call on my phone'. I called down to the desk Sgt. In less than three minutes there were five officers, including the Sgt., swarming around the cell that held both inmates. 'Come on out from under that bed,' the Sgt. said. Alex reluctantly crawled out. They cuffed him and put him in Ad Seg. He just got out about six weeks ago, and now he is in general population, not protective custody. You know everyone calls him Alex, but his real name is Andy Gump or something like that." Dan concluded.

"Hum, he said his name was Alexander Bartholomew, I wonder what he is in here for." I mused.

"I heard murder." Dan said.

"Oh? Do you know the details?" I asked.

"Yes, he found his girl with another man, he didn't kill her, but he did kill the guy she was with. Alex/Andy liked to play baseball, and had just returned from a game. He took his bat and slammed it over his head a couple times"

"Crime of passion. Well what was he doing with another inmate then?"

"A lot of them do it, then when they get out, if they ever do, they go back to a 'normal' life again," Dan kind of shrugged his shoulders.

"Huh, thanks for the info. He's in my block, but I don't see him much. He seems to go here and there a lot."

"Well, I heard he was on the Wardens Forum." Dan said.

"What does that mean?" I asked.

"I'm not sure, but when I find out I'll tell you," he half grinned at me.

"Okay. Hey have you eaten yet?" I asked.

"I just finished, but spotted the interactions of Alex and the prisoners, so I thought I'd watch for a few minutes before I went back to my assignment."

"Where are you today?"

"Covering the chapel, and of course spent time in there," he was pointing in the chow hall.

"I'll walk with you for a while before we go our separate ways." I stepped along side with Dan as we left the dining room.

"It sure is a real warm day isn't it?" he asked.

"Yup, well, I'll see you later, don't forget to tell me what you find out."

"Later."

Dan was one of the officers that were above me on the roof during the riot, that first fall of our employ. He told me he wouldn't have wanted to be in my shoes that night.

I went back to the block, and checked a few cells out while the inmates were at chow.

Soon the chow lines were returning to the block. The officers stopped the prisoners as they straggled in the block, for a physical shake down. Sometimes shanks were passed during chow, or other contraband. The Sgt. stood near while we were doing this.

I returned to my gallery and released a few prisoners for night showers, while workers returned from the kitchen. A fat guy lived up on fourth gallery. He was walking slowly up the stairs, when he hit my level he paused to catch his breath. I heard him, so I went to the end to see if anyone else was there. He was alone, and started to leave when I spotted a bulge in his middle.

"How about a shake down, buddy."

"I am not your buddy," he growled.

"Give me your package." I said.

He hesitated, and for a brief moment I felt that he was going to assault me or use a shank, then he shook his head, handed it to me, and said, "Why you doing' me that way?"

"No particular reason, just that you're busted."

He was carrying about 10 pounds of sugar for spud juice. I stored a mental note to watch his cell, or his crony's cells for spud juice in the future, and planned to share this information with the other officer on his gallery. The Sergeant said not to write a ticket, he was punished enough by my taking his sugar.

That split second could have been crucial. I looked into his big bulging eyes and realized if he decided to stick me, I was out of viewing range for the man in the turret to protect me. But, it wasn't my time yet.

Weeks were passing and I didn't have anything to report to Susan. She had tried to call me twice. I ignored it for that reason.

It would be impossible to follow him, or even make excuses to go to the control center, so I did my job and waited for the right time. I realized I would have to make him feel comfortable with me. A comfort that would finally make him want to spill the beans.

At the end of each day during my shift I would write the next days schedule for inmate movement. Out of the corner of my eye I saw Alex looking at me. I ignored him, and continued with the schedule. I was almost finished when he came right up near me and watched. I still stayed firm and acted like he was not there.

"Why are you avoiding me?" he asked.

"I didn't realize I was," I answered.

"You used to smile, and say hello, now you act as if I'm invisible."

He noticed, he cared; this may be my opening, and the opportune chance I have been waiting for.

"I have been avoiding you because I have to maintain a professional repoir between you and myself. I am trying not to be tempted." I lied.

Oh, Lord, should I have said that? I need something from him, he has kept his thoughts to himself so far, and maybe he might open up to me. I hope so.

"What? What do you mean? Have I said something to make you want to avoid me?" He asked.

"No. It really doesn't matter what I think, or what you think. I haven't given it a thought, really."

"Now you're being testy. Let's be friends."

"Okay. But, isn't it time you were locked in for final count?"

He smiled, "Ya, I'll see you tomorrow."

From that day forward it would be impossible to not speak to him. Each night before he locked in, he would find me and make small talk. 'Tell me something substantial;' I thought when he came around; I'm tired of the small talk.

It was like he read my mind, when out of the blue he said, "You know the big dark skinned inmate who lives on base, the one with the white sissy, following him around all the time?"

"Yes, I think I know which one you are referring to." I said.

"Well, he is dangerous. He will kill anyone in a flash, if he believes that anyone is guilty of snooping in his cell, he has a 'hard on' for that young officer on base."

"Now what is that supposed to mean?"

"He will do him in if he gets a chance." Alex said.

"Why?"

"Officer Sheldon shook down his cell, took something from it and wrote him a ticket for having contraband. Which gave him loss of privileges, which kept him from his job, and his sissy."

I can find out if this is true, I'll just check the tickets written in the past two weeks. If I have to ask officer Sheldon, I'll do it then, but only then. Sheldon had been arrogant with me when I busted the porter with his spud juice. He said I should not have written him a ticket.

"Okay," I said to Alex, " thanks for the tip about the guy and his sissy, I'll keep it to myself, and only say something if it is absolutely necessary."

"Thanks, I want you to be safe." He added.

How thoughtful of him. I knew this was a warning, I couldn't even trust him, let alone the big bruiser, named Bates. Bates' skin was dark; it matched his personality, dark and brooding. He scowled most of the time.

About a month later, during routine shakedowns, I stopped at prisoner Boone's cell.

"Shake down,' I said.

He sat down and put his shoes on. I immediately knew there was something in the cell. I cuffed him to the rail of the gallery.

Sure enough, I found a shank. I called down to the desk and two officers were up with me in less than a minute. Prisoner Boone was escorted to Ad Seg, without a hassle.

Sheldon was right on me. "How did you know there was a shank in there? Someone snitched him out, didn't they? You didn't know anything before you went in there, did you?'

Well, I really didn't, but his body language told me something. No one snitched him out, it was just a routine, and bottom line is he probably wanted to go to Ad Seg to feel safe; someone is probably after him, or he wouldn't have made that shank," I said.

"Officer Morgan, I need you to help push base out for chow lines. Just go down by the showers, and when the cells open, don't let them linger, get them right out of the block as fast as possible." the Sgt. said.

"Yes, sir."

The cell doors opened. Bates wasn't there. His sissy Jones came out, being pushed around by two prisoners. I saw a shank flash in the sun light; and blew my whistle. They stood dead still in their tracks. 'Big Red' went off, and I was relieved to know that the guy in the sky was watching. The shank flew across the floor, I grabbed it, as two officers tackled and cuffed the two prisoners.

Officer Sheldon to the rescue. I wondered if he would have come to Jones' rescue if he knew that Bates was after him.

The little blond sissy went to Protective Custody, the other two to Ad Seg.

Bates was livid when he heard what happened. Now he would have to find a new 'buddy,' he couldn't live without sex. He was in for killing a woman after raping her. He brutalized her and left her for dead.

I found out, after checking with the block counselor, he stalked her for a long time. He was possessed by her, and finally asked her out. She laughed in his face, which was the wrong thing to do to this personality type.

He needed to find sex, however and whenever he could. I saw him pacing in his cell, with a dark look on his face. He was ready to blow. Sometimes it sounded like he was growling. He was scary. I decided to talk to my Sgt. about him. When things died down for the evening, I went into the Sergeant's office.

"Sergeant, can I talk to you?" I asked.

"Sure, what's going on?"

"Well you know Bates, on base. His sissy is gone now and he is ready to break, he is pacing back and forth with that dark look he gets, I'm worried. I heard that he is laying for officer Sheldon, because he believes that it is Sheldon's fault that he doesn't have his sissy now. This is the corrupt mind at work."

"You're right. I'll see what I can do," He said.

"Thanks, sir."

The next day when I came on shift, there was a new inmate in Bates' cell; Bates was shipped out on the 'snow train' up north in the mountain country.

Chapter 31

"Hello," I answered a ringing phone.

"It's Susan."

"Hey, you caught me, we have been playing phone tag, haven't we?"

"We sure have," Susan replied. "When can we get together?"

" How about next Monday, my day off, or I could come in early if it is urgent."

"No, Monday is fine. Same place?" she said.

"So far no one has noticed us," I said.

"Okay, see you then. Around one thirty?"

"Sounds good."

My weekend off was great. It was good to be with family, having Sunday Dinner after church. How relaxing it was to share the news about my grand children's' progress in school, sometimes we would go fishing at the nearby lake, catch some blue gill, and those tiny sunfish. The boys loved it! Soon it was dusk and time to go home after a long wonderful day. This day was particularly great because Ralph returned and was only gone when there was a long trip.

Monday came fast; washed clothes, hung the bedding out to get outdoors smell, showered, and slipped on a mint colored shorts set and left in time to be at The House of Chin at precisely one thirty. My short-cropped dark brown hair was dry by the time I arrived. As I glanced over the parking lot I saw Susan driving her Mercedes in right behind me.

I smiled at her meeting to walk in together, "Hi, good timing," I said.

"Didn't you notice? I was parked along your highway, waiting, when you passed me, I slipped the car into gear and followed you."

"Ha, I was so engrossed in the news on the radio that I didn't see you. Some doctor said after his research over one year, he believes that pickles cause cancer. He was live, and getting calls in over the radio to discuss the pros and cons on whether it was true or not."

"Oh well, were all going to die from something," Susan said.

Isn't that the truth?

"I want something light today, I'm cutting back, trying to lose about ten pounds, because my slacks are getting tight," I said as I tried to get my thumb in the waist.

"Well, I'm hungry, so I'm getting the usual, Moo Choo Chicken, with cashews, and two Spring Rolls on the side."

"I'll have Beef and Broccoli without the rice. And hot tea."

"Let's talk about Alex. Have you found out anything yet?"

"Uh, well, he is on the Warden Forum, moves around a lot, I understand that he takes the prisoners gripes, writes them down on his clip board, and meets with the Warden to discuss them with him."

"Does he tell you what the gripes are?"

"Hey, you're a Deputy Warden, don't you go to the meetings?" I asked.

"No, I haven't gone. The warden has not asked me to any of them."

"That's strange. I find it hard to believe that you are not included when the 'forum' meets. But there is another thing I want to tell you about."

I told her about being warned about Bates, and finally went to the Sgt. the next day Bates was gone. Transferred out.

"So Alex told you that he was dangerous?"

"Yes, he said he didn't want me to get hurt. I really thought that if anyone got hurt it would be the base officer. He's the one who busted him, and sent him to Ad. Seg. for a month."

"So, Alex would care if you got hurt?" she brushed the base officers safety off as if it was nothing. She was leaning forward, like she thought she was on to something. Her wheels were turning; I could see it in her eyes.

"It appears that way. He could say that just to make me feel like I owe him something. I have been testy, and have not let him think one way or the other about how I feel."

"So, has he told you anything else?" she asked.

"No, and you know, this has been trying. It seems to be taking a lot out of me trying to milk anything out of him. I have tried to avoid him, to make him ask why, and he did ask why, yet he still does not spill the beans. What in particular do you think he is doing?"

"Give him time, he will," she said.

"Good, can't wait. What do you think he is doing?" I repeated.

"Right now I think he is a 'mule,' carrying dope to this one, then carrying money to that one."

"Like who?" I asked.

"He's the Wardens boy isn't he?" she said.

"Maybe. How does he do it without getting caught?"

"That's what you're doing. You are going to find out, tell me, and then, you drop him, and I will take care of the rest."

We finished eating, and made small talk about the weather pickles caused cancer.

Why hasn't the warden asked her to the meetings with the prisoner? Was he involved with the trafficking of dope? She worked at the school at the time of Mayberry's death. Did she suspect anything or anyone other than the prisoner who was doing life for the crime? Had she heard the same story from the prisoners, that the administration, and on down were involved? 'Just throw in the keys' and we'll have a great time, someone new every time. But, you had to play ball. Mayberry didn't play ball. In fact she probably ran unto two or more having a great time. What did Susan know? Was this what the FBI wanted? Was the twelve reporting, and watching like I was, all in the same prison, one of the largest walled prisons in the world? I felt alone. I CAN'T TRUST ANYONE. Not even Susan; who knew more about me than I did her.

Porter Sam Powers said she was very close to a porter upstairs, when she worked at the Prison School. He was always gossiping, and waiting for my reaction. He could have been telling the truth about what really happened to that female officer; after all he was transferred out shortly after he told me about it. Or was he one of the twelve?

I realized it was time to talk to Alex everyday.

Chapter 32

Hello, what's this? Officer Brown talking to her favorite prisoner? Is her hand in the cell, through the bars? She doesn't see her partner coming towards her.

I leaped two steps at a time up the stairs to get there and witness anything necessary. She was so engrossed with what she was doing that she didn't see me walking quickly and quietly toward her, and she jumped when she did finally see me.

"Oh, Hi, what are you doing up here?" she asked me.

About the same time officer Gillman approached, and overheard what she asked me.

"Can I be a witness?" he asked. Cocking his head to one side with that silly look.

I almost laughed out loud.

"Oh, the Sgt. asked me to relieve you for a minute, to discuss a ticket you wrote, I think," I said.

She looked puzzled, and left the gallery. I looked in Nathaniel Johnston's cell casually, taking everything in. Gillman was talking to the prisoner. He had a gift for gab, this was helpful, and it gave me time to quickly peruse the cell. Then it hit me!

"Hey, Gillman, let's do a routine, " I looked at the prisoner. The big man in the Mores couldn't look me in the eye, his eyes were on the floor.

Gillman said, " Sure. Here buddy, back against the bars, so I can cuff you." Johnston backed to the bars and let Gillman cuff him. I unlocked the cell and Johnston came out and stood leaning against the rail with officer Gillman.

I went in and, searched all over; desk drawer, mattress, slits in the mattress, under the bed, sink, under the sink. Then my eyes locked on a vent hole about three inches in diameter. It was plugged. I pulled out the plug. Out came at least eight ounces of marijuana wrapped and encased with a 'rubber.'

Do I flush it? No, that's my law on second gallery. This was on 3rd gallery. Did Johnston see me find it? No, I don't think he did. He is acting too normal. He's a cool one if he did. Judgment call; do I keep it and tell the Sgt. later? Or do I show Gillman? I'll have to show Gillhead and go from there. I shoved the plug back in the vent hole; the prophylactic encased package went into my pocket.

"Hey, Gillman, come her," I said.

Johnston was talking to his 'homie' in the next cell.

"Look," I said in lower tones, "It was in the vent, with a plug over it," his eyes widened.

"Okay, Johnston, were done for now, you can go back in your cell," he said.

Gillman took off the cuffs after he was locked back in. We weren't even to the end of the gallery, when I heard slamming, and cursing. Gillman was chuckling to himself.

"I'll handle this since it is my gallery, and you be my witness, okay?" Gillman said.

"Sure."

Do I mention I believe that officer Julia Brown gave it to him? No I'll save it for DW Lorenzo. Besides I couldn't prove that when her hand was in the cell she was handing him something.

"I want to talk to you, Officer Morgan," said Sergeant Rogers." What were you thinking when you sent officer Brown down here, telling her I wanted to talk to her about something? Don't put me on a spot like that again, you hear? What happened up there?"

" I had a hunch, and knew I had to follow through. I'm sorry if I was out of my bounds. But it did pay off. Gillman is writing the ticket right now, he has the evidence. There was marijuana, a lot of it, in Johnston's cell."

"Okay, this time. I picked up on something and went with it when officer Brown came down. I can cover for your actions, good job. You're a good cop."

I took in a deep breath; this was all I wanted to hear. The Sgt. was a good boss.

"I hear you hooked up Johnston," said Alex.

"Who told you that?"

"I hear everything in this cell block. He wants to complain to the warden."

"Well, complain he can. He knows that he wasn't supposed to be messing with that stuff. If he was on my gallery it would have gone down the tube, but he isn't."

"You're hard, you could get hurt doing this kind of thing."

"Are you threatening me?" I asked, looking straight into his eyes.

"No, I'm just saying that… oh, forget it." He shrugged.

"I understand. I know that it was a judgement call, and I had to decide quickly how to treat this situation. Officer Gillman agreed that it was the thing to do. I shouldn't be discussing this with you, but I think you will understand more since I did."

I can't help but believe he is one of 'us.' The things he says. If he isn't he is clever and dangerous. He could be more dangerous than Bates. With Bates you knew where he was coming from. This guy is playing both sides, or at least he is trying to.

"I understand more than you may well guess. We need room to breath, I won't be talking to you anymore," he said.

"Oh, why, can't you handle realizing that I have a job to do and I will?" I asked.

"Yes, I know you will."

I never felt as alone as I did right then. The bottom fell out. I felt I knew what he was doing; he's being pulled between being a 'mule' and knowing right from wrong. How will you tell the DW that the 'subject' won't talk to me because I busted a prisoner? What is the connection between, officer Brown, and Alexander? Why did he get so upset? He could realize what would happen if I caught him! This is too heavy, if it's true the administration is behind all the drug trafficking, then the FBI has to be on the other end wanting to know who, what, where and when. I was in deeper than I wanted to be.

I started experiencing extreme pain in my chest. I thought I was having a heart attack. I told myself to calm down, and take a deep breath.

Hang in there. Do your job. Think straight.

On my way home I thought about it, and realized I was in a jam. I wanted to please the DW; I respected her and believed that what I was doing to help the FBI, and her, was 'being a good officer.' Being a good officer was the ultimate reason for everything I did. So I kept thinking how I could be able to continue watching Alex, and keep giving information to Susan. I was almost home when the pains in my chest came back again. I pulled over to the side of the road, opened the window, and took a few deep breaths. After what seemed a very long time, the pains subsided. I drove home with my favorite Gospel tape in the tape player, and sang along. Soon, I was in my 'I'm home and everything in my life is wonderful' mode.

The next day I called my doctor and made an appointment to see her. She didn't have an opening until December 12th, six weeks away. I scheduled the appointment and marked it on my calendar.

My next phone call was to Susan Lorenzo. She didn't answer, so I left a message to see about lunch soon. I knew she would call within one day.

I went into work with a positive attitude. Yard was in process when I arrived. When they came in I had to shake down the inmates as they passed. This meant to check, arms, legs, trunk, and never forget the small of their back. This is where they often taped a shank. There are usually six officers, including me, routinely shaking them down as they entered the block. The yard crew was pushing them in, following them at a distance. About halfway through the lines, Alex came up to me and turned his back for me to shake him down.

He must have thought things over and came to the conclusion that he shouldn't have said what he did.

I quickly did the shake down and said, "Next."

If he wanted to talk it would have to be later.

After my lunch break I stopped at the Sgt. desk, and asked for an update, on anything new since I left the block. Sgt. Rogers said to follow him into his office.

"Sit down," he pointed to the chair across from him. "I have something to tell you. I want you to hear it first from me."

"Yes?"

"I'm being transferred into "C" Block," he hesitated, waiting for it to sink in. "I want you to go with me."

I would rather work for him than any other Sergeant in the whole system, but for now I had to stay with this block to be 'near' my 'subject'.

"I can't tell you why, but at this time I cannot transfer with you."

He looked down at the desk, "Okay, I won't ask you why, but if you change your mind, let me know."

"When will you be leaving?" I asked.

"The first of the month."

"Good, so we have a couple weeks before you are gone," I smiled at him and left his office. His expression was disappointment with concern.

The next day he handed me the following Memorandum:

'Well people, we've had a good run, however, all good races must end. I'm leaving 'A' Block, effective 12-1-91. I will be working in 'C' Block. I hear this block is supposed to give me a challenge.

When I first arrived here in March 1990, I was assigned as the only Sgt. in 'A' block. They had previously been assigning two sergeants; one for the east and one for the west side. With some success, I have managed to surround myself with quality staff, which has enhanced the day-to-day activities of this block. This block is no longer the block <u>not to work; this block is the place to work.</u> This I believe is a direct result of <u>you</u>.

I would like to thank each of you for doing such a good job. The experience has and will be a memorable one, for some time to come. I will always answer YES with pride, when I am asked if I ever worked in 'A' block. You come into tough situations everyday, yet you handle each situation with professionalism. You should all be proud of your accomplishments and proud that you are a part of the 'A' block team.

Again thanks for everything and I hope to work with you all again someday. Take care and good luck!!!

I went up to my gallery heavy hearted. I couldn't hold the disappointment of Sergeant leaving for long on my heart. I swallowed hard to fight back the tears that wanted to emerge out of my eyes and roll down my cheeks.

It was time for showers. I checked my list to see which ones were scheduled for this time of day, and unlocked them. They would say 'okay,' 'I don't want on,' or 'pass.' Alex was talking to someone on down the gallery. While my partner followed the six down to base to the showers I walked on down to see who he was talking to.

"Hey, how you doin?" I asked nonchalantly.

"Okay. I guess, just talking to my homie here, you know Jim Stark, he paints, everywhere in the prison. Even paints in the warden's office. Right Jim?"

Jim cleared his throat, "Err, yes, I have painted in there, put in some long hours."

"Well, I can call you money bags from now on," I said.

"They do already, sho' 'nuf. Don't mean I do tho'," Jim said.

"Don't tell me you spend it as soon as you make it, do you Jim?" I asked.

"I save it up."

"That's good."

I completed my round and went back to the south end of the gallery, near the gun post wall, to waited for straggling shower inmates, to return. As they returned, I would lock them in and let six more out again until all were showered.

'Andy Gump' what a plain name. No wonder he tagged the Alexander Bartholomew name and claimed it. Alias, that's what it was; he probably wanted to feel important, who knows?

Alex followed me to the end of the gallery. I leaned against the railing, facing outwards towards base, and he did the same. The officer in the gun turret could see both of us, which gave me a secure feeling.

"That guy, you know, Jim, he is safe," he said.

"What do you mean?" I asked.

"If I'm not here, he will help you."

"Help me what?"

This isn't going well. What if the man in the sky reads lips?

"I mean, I've tried to warn you many times about the Moors; about the guy on base, Bates; about being too hard. I may not always be here, so if I'm gone, what I'm saying is that you can trust him."

"Okay, thanks."

Shit, I can't trust anyone; Alex included. Why should I trust Jim? Well, it could be something I could remember if needed, for the future.

I couldn't help but wonder about Alex and Jim - if they had something in common. Did they know everything about each other? I had to remain silent and watch.

More prisoners were coming back from the showers, one whistled at Alex. He said 'thanks'. Which makes me think he really is a sissy. He was grinning at me.

He is talking to me again. This is good, but the Moore's could be a problem. Officer Brown also could be a problem if she did indeed bring in the dope I found in Johnston's cell.

One night the count to go to the library was over twenty, so I had to escort them over and stay during the one-hour period. Once we arrived, I sat with the library officer in the hall, until half time when the prisoners could come out of the library and smoke or go to the restroom.

Otis Williams is a prisoner from my gallery. He is a tall skinny black man, a member of the Moors, who works in the kitchen. He often tried to make conversation with me, I was always brief and to the point. Once he said he would like to take me out when he got out. He didn't like my response, but he kept trying never the less. Half time was over for library. All the prisoners were returning, so I followed the prisoners back into the library. Suddenly I felt someone in my space, breathing down my back. I turned and Williams was one foot from me. I looked straight in his eyes and said, "Where did you come from?"

"I was in the bathroom."

I motioned for him to get in front of me, and made a mental note to make sure from now on to watch him close. I never found out what he is in for, but most in 'A' Block are in for murder, with life sentences. His action that evening made my already intense dislike for him increase.

Williams loved to bring food back from kitchen duty. Sometimes he would sell hotdogs and chips to his cronies.

I always remembered the golden rule of the prison; do not trust anyone. True to form, after coming back from my lunch break, I found officer Steve Sewell in front of Williams' cell. Sewell reached into his pocket and gave Williams a small square package. He looked up and realized I saw him give it to him. I didn't say anything. Just watched as I passed by, finishing my round making my way back to the south end of the gallery.

Sewell followed and said that he just gave him a jazz tape. I couldn't trust his judgment.

"Really, I didn't know."

He just looked at me acting a little irate. "I'm not giving up my job of 18 years over just a jazz tape, and an over-ambitious co-worker."

Is a threat or a statement? I asked him looking directly in his eyes. "Listen. It doesn't matter. Let it go, okay?" I said.

"Okay."

Later, after final count, at 9:10 p.m., I went in for my usual talk with Sgt. Rogers, soon it would be the last after he transferred out to "C" block.

Suddenly, Sewell burst in and said, and "May I face my accuser?"

We both said, "What?"

He looked from the Sgt. to me and back again, and said, "Oh, nothing." Looking sheepish, he left the office.

"What was that all about, or should I ask?"

"Maybe later. Not now, Sergeant Rogers, it's really nothing."

Chapter 33

I usually reached my driveway by 11:15 each night after leaving work. The first thing I do is turn on the TV, take off my shoes, undress, take a shower, and slump onto the couch. It takes up to two hours each night to wind down.

When the phone rang the next morning at seven, I was not ready to be awake.

"Hello?"

"It's Susan, where have you been? Trying to get you is almost impossible."

"Really busy. Lots to tell you though. Want to get together?"

"That's why I called, we do need to talk. How about breakfast at that restaurant in you're town where we met for that Women in Corrections Meeting?"

"Sure, what time?" I asked.

"I'm here now, how long will it take you?"

"Fifteen minutes."

I splashed water on my face to wake up, slip into jeans and a sweatshirt, grab my purse, and jump in the car.

"Hi," I said as I breezed into the Wheel Inn café.

"Hi, tell me all. Tell me about Officer Brown, and resident Williams, and our 'subject.'"

How did she know about Brown and Williams? I told her everything, right down to the fact that Sgt. Rogers was being transferred into 'C' Block. By the time that I was finished I had, put away two large pancakes, and three strips of bacon, washed down with four cups of coffee.

"Okay, here's what I want you to d. Continue pumping Alex for information, find out what that painter knows; he may be helpful. I also want you to watch officer Brown's partner, you know the one who wrote the ticket on the marijuana you found?"

"Right, you may not realize this, but I have been having chest pains, I'm going to the doctor next month."

I changed the subject. I could wager he was cleaner than Monday's wash.

"Oh, Anne, everyone who works there has chest pains."

"Really?" I asked.

"It just comes with the territory. Breathe deep and talk yourself out of it."

"Easy to say, but I have done just that."

"See, it works every time. Is there anything else you want to tell me?"

"Well, yes, this one prisoner has been stalking me. He has been fresh with his conversation, always saying he wants to take me out. I want to puke every time he says anything to me. I believe he is dirty. But who isn't in there?" I said. "There is more, he is a Moor, and he steals from the kitchen to sell hot dogs and chips to his cronies."

"Tell me about the stalking."

I told her about the night at the library.

"He was actually waiting for me to go first then came up behind. I could feel his breath on my neck. I think he was trying to scare me, or was debating as to whether he should do me in."

"What did you say his name is?" Susan asked.

"Otis Williams, he lives on my gallery. "

"I'll check into this guy."

"Well, I appreciate it, but please don't put yourself out."

155

"Don't worry, it can be done easily, we'd better call it a day, it's well past ten. You work today don't you?"

"Sure do, I have to wash my uniform too. I'll get my groceries on the way home from work."

"Keep in touch, and be careful. I didn't tell you that my husband is home from one of his trips, always here or there doing a tri-athalon. He will be home when I get there, so I'd better get something nice and healthy for supper."

"I didn't know he was busy with the sports events, is this global?"

"Yes, he flies everywhere for competition. Well I'd better go, see you later."

"Okay, have a good one."

This is getting old. I'm getting tired of snooping around on my job. I'm laying my life on the line, just to feel I am a good officer. If the warden, or someone is involved with dope smuggling in the prison, I could be killed too. On the other hand, Genevieve hinted that one of her crew is bringing in cocaine. Someone wants the monopoly on all the trafficking. Susan may want to know whom the small boys are to get rid of them and be the chief. Who can I trust? I'm just tired of the whole game.

Chapter 34

The next day at work when taking my first round, the prisoner in the third cell was happy as a lark because he was going home today.

"You are?" I said. I hadn't heard anything about it. He was yelling to his cronies and giving up his possessions. He asked me for a bag to pack his clothes up along with his personals. The only items he would leave is his state issued clothing and shoes.

"Okay, when I go down to base, I'll get a duffle bag out of the storeroom for you."

I went down to the desk, on base, and asked Sgt. Moses about him leaving. She replaced Sgt. Rogers.

She said, "He isn't going anywhere. He has to many out-of-place tickets, girl, he can't even go to yard."

"He is asking for a packing bag and is giving all his possessions to his cronies."

"Go up there and tell him that he isn't going home."

"Yes, ma'm."

"Mr. Blood, you are not scheduled to go home today."

"When then, tomorrow?"

"No not tomorrow."

"What do you mean? I gave everything away, I have to go, and it's on this slip. It says the date here."

The slip was a paper that was given him when he first came in, showing his ERD.

I looked at the slip; today was his early release date.

"Oh, this is your early release date. This means if you have been on good behavior, could go before the parole board and then if you were released, you would go home then."

He slumped down on his bed, and said he wanted to die.

By the nine o'clock count he was talking some strange stuff; like he was dead, and he didn't care. I went to the Sgt. and she talked to him.

She said in low tones, "go call the mini amb, he will have to go for psychiatric evaluation." I had never seen anyone break down so fast before. I felt so bad for him. When the ambulance came and took him from the block, I ran to our restroom, shut the door and cried my eyes out.

Am I cracking up? I felt so sorry for young Blood, he really thought he was going home. So young, yet so much in trouble, and not mature enough to understand.

The next day I wakened early and worked outdoors for most of the morning.

The phone was ringing as I went through the backdoor.

"Hello?"

"YOU'RE DEAD."

"Who is this?" the phone went dead.

I had nothing to lose, I was dead. I walked into work with a chip on my shoulder. I spoke very little to any of the officers during role call, went straight up to my gallery, made a round, and stopped at Williams cell, it was empty. I opened the barred door and went straight to the sink where water was left trickling on his food, hotdogs and cheese, to keep it cold. I took it and threw it on base. Next I took his extra mattress off the bed and threw it on base, he was issued only one, and the second was contraband. I threw everything that he was not supposed to have over the rail it went to base below.

I stormed on down to the porters cell and did the same thing. I found more spud juice, and flushed it down the toilet. I threw out anything he wasn't supposed to have.

A white prisoner was complaining that he wanted to go to Protective Custody because he is afraid of Chet Hester, the prisoner in the cell next to him. I went into Hester's cell and hit it hard too. Hester had a Koran. His Koran was hollowed out in a square shape and filled with some white powder. I took the hallowed out Koran and the white substance straight to the Sgt's desk, while Hester went to the 'hole.'

I cleaned house on just enough prisoners so that whoever called me and said 'your dead,' will wish they hadn't.

Williams returned from work. The entire block heard him screaming, "I'll kill that white honky bitch."

With my back to the gallery, I smiled inside.

My life was threatened, and I almost went berserk. I really needed my two days off. That was the closest I had come to quitting my job and going on unemployment.

Who would call me and threaten my life? Who had my phone number? I made quite a few people mad at me, including Officer Brown. I cut in on her 'man' and their little dope deals. I had caught Officer Sewell giving what he said was a jazz tape to Otis Williams. He could have called and said 'you're dead,' but he doesn't have the backbone to do it. Had word gone as far as the warden's office? Alex was there every time I was doing my job; he knew I wouldn't back down. Did he say something to the wrong person? There are many prisoners that want to get me, and they could if they were that serious. There are more that a few officers that crossed the line on sexual harassment. But I never said anything about them to anyone.

Then who? My chest began to get that crushing feeling again, tightening up like someone had a grip on my heart. I wanted to pass out from the chest pain; I missed that doctor's appointment I made. I am still adapting to the new Sgt. She moved me to another gallery. There are two prisoners on that gallery with AIDS. One is a sissy, called 'Ms. Chocolate,' the other was a junkie, who had it before going to prison on drug charges.

I called Dr. Blankenhorn to try to reschedule my appointment for next week, hoping I wouldn't have a heart attack before then. I felt rested enough from my weekend to be ready for anything when I returned to work on Tuesday. It really was good to be off, I did as little as possible.

Chapter 35

The warden paced back and forth in his office. He obviously has something on his mind of great importance: Kincaid. Kincaid is a good officer; does his job, is never absent, keeps to himself and doesn't ask questions, which is what worries the warden.

Warden Hale knows Kincaid car-pools to work me. He knows he'll have to talk to Kincaid before too long. It was two months since the chicken delivery. He had to depend on Kincaid to help get the white packages to the right storage place. Kincaid had been cool, but for how long?

The little white bags that were stuffed in the chickens, rested in a fake wall behind his clothes closet where rifles were stored in the olden days, in case of riots. New shipments replaced them twice.

Warden Hale called on the intercom to his secretary, Marlow Malinski, "Marlow , would you get Kincaid on the phone for me?"

"Yes, Warden Hale."

He rubbed his hands together, leaned back in his chair, and waited. The phone rang.

"Connecting Kincaid now sir," Marlow said.

"We need to talk, Kincaid," Warden Hale said to officer Kincaid.

"Yes sir, when."

"I'd like you to come to my office during your break, I'll be leaving at five."

"I'll be up in 15 minutes."

Kincaid wondered what was up. He and the warden usually met at the delivery dock, and used code words like 'get the boat we're going fishing'. He went to the wardens' office. Marlow Malinski smiled at him and said, "I'll let him know you're here, Kincaid."

"Officer Kincaid is here, sir." She said into the intercom.

"Ah, come in Kincaid. Have a seat," he said motioning to the seat across the desk from him.

"You wanted to talk to me, Warden Hale?"

"Yes," he paused, " I'm concerned about your complete loyalty. I have to know that you are not telling anyone about our, err, the business we do together."

"Of course, I told you I would never tell, you pay me too well. Why would I give up that nice little nest egg over stupidity?"

"Others have slipped before. So naturally you are suspect," he started to walk around his office.

" I swear, I'll never tell anyone anything." Kincaid's eyes were evasive as if he confided something in someone, but Hale didn't seem to notice.

"Well, I'm happy to see that I can trust you Kincaid. We'll keep in touch and I'll let you know when I need you again. Okay, buddy?"

"Yes, sir, you can count on me," he said as he got up to leave.

Hale slapped him on the back and smiled.

Kincaid left the office with a fake smile on his face, but he knew it wasn't convincing.

That evening he was leaving the main entry after his shift and decided to get a cup of coffee before the trip home.

 The coffee machine was in the hall next to the warden's office. The lights were on, so he stepped into the outer office and found Marlow typing.

"Working late?" he asked.

"Yes, I could use some coffee too, I'm getting tired. Would you get me some?"

He set his coffee on her desk and said, "Sure, be right back."

Hale said 'we have to get rid of Kincaid. He is dangerous to our plan.' This was the opportunity Hale meant, 'if it comes up.' It wouldn't take long to open the capsule and drain the contents in Kincaid's coffee while he was out. She heard the doorknob turning. She quickly snapped the cap over the Styrofoam cup.

"You are a doll, really. Thank you so much. How much do I owe you?" She knew, but wanted him to say 'nothing.'

"Nothing."

"Are you alone tonight, or is officer Morgan with you?"

"Alone, this is her day off."

She knew that too, but was just making small talk. It takes exactly 10 minutes for the pill to take effect. Which would get him about three miles down the road. It would look like he fell asleep at the wheel again, like he did about eight months ago.

She smiled at him while he left the room, and said, "Good night."

Killing was easy for Marlow, this wasn't her first time either.

The next day on my way to work, I was thinking about, how I cleaned out three cells, and how it hit Otis Williams the hardest. I remembered how mad he was, banging his cupboard doors, screaming, and calling me the worst thing he could think of at the time.

At role call we were told that Officer Kincaid fell to sleep at the end of Florence Street, and was hit by a car full of teenagers, coming home from the game. They ran into him as he crossed the street without trying to stop. Witnesses said he was killed instantly. Two of the school kids were hospitalized: one with a broken leg and the other with head wounds.

My heart wrenched. He never did anything bad to anyone, I thought.

I walked into my block only to have Sgt. Moses call me over to her desk.

"You're wanted in Internal Investigations, I'll have someone cover for you until you get back," she said.

"What is it about?"

"Girl, I couldn't tell you. They just said for you to come over as soon as you arrived."

"Okay, thanks, Sgt. I'll talk to you when I get back."

I left the block wondering what it was about. It could be anything. Once before I was asked repeat to what I told the teachers and librarian to I & I, but they just wanted to thank me for taking time to talk to them. I wondered if it had something to do with Officer Kincaid? I didn't know anything, except what he told in complete confidence?

I walked into I & I and said, "Hi, I'm Officer Morgan, I understand that Mr. Godfry wants to speak to me?"

"Yes, let me tell him that you are here." his secretary responded.

I waited, while she went into his office to let him know I was there.

"You may go right in. I will be joining you to witness what is said."

"Hello, Mr. Godfry. I understand you want to talk to me."

"Yes, I have a 'memo' from prisoner Otis Williams. He sent it yesterday morning. Please read it and tell me what, if any, of it is true?"

The memo read:

'Officer Morgan is having oral sex with a prisoner every night at nine o'clock. She does final rounds then goes down to his gallery and leans against the bars and has oral sex.' Signed, Otis Williams.'

"What! None of this memo is true," I said outraged.

163

"Do you care to elaborate on it?"

"I'm saying that it is a bold-faced lie."

"Then, what are you doing at that time of night after your last round?" Godfry asked.

"Writing tickets, talking to the Sgt. about the days incidents."

"And you can prove this?"

"Of course I can."

"Do you go to any prisoners cell at that time of night for any reason?"

"I have from time to time, but not for more than three minutes, and certainly not for oral sex.'"

"Who do you go to talk to?"

"The block rep for the Warden's Forum."

"And you have never had sex, or never did anything sexual towards him."

"Never!" The pig, I thought. I felt like spitting, to clean the sick taste in my mouth.

"Alright, officer Morgan, I accept your candidacy. We'll take care of this incident ourselves."

"Wait, have you thought why Williams wrote this about me?" I asked Godfry.

"No, is there a reason?"

" I had just cleaned out his cell last week, there was contraband; an extra mattress, left over food from the mess hall, so I and wrote him up. This is retaliation. He is a total creep, he stalked me in the library, oh well forget it," I said.

"No that is what I wanted to hear. Will you write a memo about that incident? I will need it for the record."

"Yes sir, I will write it and return it as soon as possible." I said.

"We'll look into this and get it settled. Thank you again. You are dismissed." He rose and shook my hand.

Ralph and I went to Kincaid's memorial. His family was there. His mother was a tall lanky gray haired lady, stooped over, with a long coat. Kincaid had six brothers all looking very similar to each other. They had Kincaid cremated.

We didn't stick around after the memorial. Some of the officers who lived in the area were there also.

The warden was pacing back and forth in his office. The decision to get rid of anyone who was jeopardizing his flow of dope money has come up.

"We have a problem, I would have talked to you before but I just realized what is happening." Hale said.

He was speaking to an older gentleman, officer Drake, who worked inside, and knew because he was one of the suppliers, just exactly what the warden was talking about. He was aware that a certain officer was busting his pushers, before the dope could be distributed, and moreover, before any money could be made.

Drake was in over his head. He really didn't want to be a part of this, but Hale held a secret over his head. Drake was caught with a prisoner in the catwalks. Hale personally took care of the incident, and it wasn't reported to the 'higher-ups.'

Hale, on the other hand, needed Drake. Drake had connections. He could charm a snake. Business always went smoothly with his hand in it.

"You know Alex, here, he is the liaison between the prisoners and us." Hale said to Drake.

"No, I am just finding out this piece of information. So what exactly are you going to do about the problem?" Drake asked, notably stressing 'you.'

"Officer Morgan busts the prisoners every time we get the stuff into the prison. She's a good officer, but I've had enough of her meddling. It's time something was done about her. We've done it before." Hale said.

"What do you think we can do and get away with it?" asked Drake.

"Pin something on her, so she has to quit or be fired. Murder is too dirty, and we almost didn't get away with it the last time." Mike Hale, the warden said.

"I don't want any part of this," Alex said.

"Don't worry, we'll set you up nice; move you to another facility, anything you want." Hale said.

Alex's mind was swirling.

They sent the killer of the other female officer, where no one could get him, and he was in a motel surroundings.

I don't want to go there. It's like a fortress, even if I did have everything I wanted: plushy cell, colored TV, Alex thought.

"I can't guarantee anything. I'll try, but you know it's going to be hard to get to her. She is no dummy. It's like she has a sixth sense," Alex said.

"You can handle it, Alex, we have confidence in you." The two men nodded at each other in affirmation.

"Okay, do you have a 'message' for me to take back to the block?" Alex asked.

"Right, here is a nice white package for the man on third, he can get it out to the right ones because of his work location right now." Alex took it and made for the door.

"Hey, put it up your ass before you leave, eh dummy?" Hale said.

The door shut, and Hale immediately said, "We need to get rid of him soon too, he is getting sloppy."

"That can be arranged too." Drake said.

Alex leaned against the wall, and overheard them talking. He knew he needed to see about a transfer immediately. After delivering the package to the man on third gallery he went directly to the councilors office to see about a transfer. If I can get out of here before she gets back, I won't have to 'ice' Morgan,' he thought.

He walked hurriedly through the control center, past the checkpoint gates and directly to the block counselor's office. The office was empty. He entered and blurted it out.

"Hi, Mr. Malcolm, I need to be transferred immediately, to avoid a problem that I can't discuss. Believe me, it is serious, or I wouldn't be here," Alex said.

"Okay, I can do this, but I'll have to tell them something," counselor Malcolm responded.

"You know I am on the Warden's Forum, just say that I know too much and have to leave before something happens between the Moors and the Milanics, and that my life is in jeopardy," Alex said.

"All right, but the soonest I can arrange that is tomorrow," said the counselor.

"That will work. Thank you, but I'll be holding my breath until then."

"I'll take care of you," the councilor said.

Alex walked out of the counselor's office thinking, *'she returns to work tomorrow. With luck I'll be gone by then.'*

As I walked into the block the next day, the Sgt. called me aside and told me, they shipped Williams out on the 'snow train'. Which meant he was transferred to the mountains, in the northern part of the state.

"Good news." I smiled.

What a relief! No more stalking, no more harassment from his demented fantasy about dating me, no more wondering if Officer Sewell really was dirty and bringing in something to Williams. I is over for him, but now who is lurking in the shadows, just waiting to be the new mule? The fact that Williams wouldn't be making money, selling dope could be a reason to do me in. He could leave instructions with the Moors or Melanics to do it.

"They're shipping another prisoner tomorrow, too. It's the warden's boy, Andy Gump. You know Alex Bartholemew."

Shit! How did this happen? I'm relieved I won't have to watch him any more, but nervous because Susan will be upset that he's gone. My chest started to hurt. I tried to talk myself out of it by deep breathing. Relax, I told myself, and get your job done.

"No kidding, why? He has a problem too?" I asked her nonchalantly.

"The counselor left instructions for the day shift Sergeant. He didn't leave details. The transfer was submitted last night and followed through tomorrow morning," Sgt Moses answered.

I thought a moment, and said, "Well, I need to get to work. Thanks for the update, Sergeant."

I went to my gallery and started the first round. A prisoner stood near his bars with his hands at his sides and blood dripping from his fingers. Looking closely I realized he had cut his arms from one end to the other. He had hacked across his arms every inch or so with a broken light bulb.

I went down to base and said to call the mini ambulance, and told the Sgt. what happened. She said to let him stay where he was until the ambulance arrived. Considering that he could have AIDS, I agreed.

I released the prisoners who were on work duty, told them what was happening, but to ignore it. They continued on their way and went right past him to their job. The ambulance came and fortunately I didn't have to escort him to the hospital. I had the gallery porter clean up his cell, while my partner watched.

With this incident, a report to write, and my routine shift work, I didn't have time to think about Alex leaving. It was close to last count when I finished writing the prisoners schedule for the next day on the chalkboard. Alex came up to me and handed me a note folded up so tiny, no one could see it.

I slipped it into my pocket and walked directly towards the desk, saying, "I hear you will be leaving us tomorrow."

"Yes, but I'm not sure where to. It will be sometime tomorrow though."

"Well, I wish you the best of luck at the new place. This was sudden wasn't it? What will the warden do?" I asked.

"Oh, he'll find someone to be his patsy," Alex said.

"What do you mean by that?"

He looked up and realized we were out of hearing distance and said, "More than you want to know. I kept him happy for over a year. Now he will have to find someone else to carry the good news and the bad news back and forth from him and his cronies to my block and to the prisoners that are involved."

"Oh, I see. Well, I appreciate all you did to help the prisoners, and listening to their complaints, and keeping a good attitude, and all."

He shook his head back and forth, like he didn't think I knew what he was trying to say. I acted dumb.

"Remember what I said about the painter," he said.

"Okay, sure I will."

I never did go to the painter for help. Although I did watch him and his contacts, wondering if he was also a mule.

The following may be irrelevant, but it is one of many ways prisoners could bring in dope. Many are caught, yet many more slipped by the eyes of the officers.

One day I was assigned to the visiting room; the crew was short, and the captain needed me to cover it. A 'femmie' looking prisoner had a visitor. They sat close, but it didn't appear she was his girlfriend, possibly his sister. They were sitting very close. I made rounds around the visiting room. I motioned to the two officers on the front gate, speaking in low tones, 'please help keep an eye on the two, they are acting suspicious'. They said they would watch and warn the control center officer to focus the cameras on the two. The prisoner began to squirm in his seat. The camera zeroed in on them.

The officers took the prisoner into the room for a strip and cavity shake down. He refused. So the officer in charge told him to dress. Then they taped his pant legs and waist shut, and escorted him to the hospital. The doctor had to probe the package out; it was three inches in diameter and one foot long. The 'mule' was escorted to Ad. Seg.

There are more stories similar to this one, yet only one of many ways dope is infiltrated in the prison.

I left Alex and walked directly to the restroom, with the note in my pocket.

I knew I had to read the note and get rid of it in case anyone saw him give it to me. I went into the bathroom and locked the door. Pulling out the note I unfolded it and read, 'Please let my sister know that I have been transferred out, this is her phone number.' I tore out the number, put it in my billfold, and ripped the remaining part of the note into tiny pieces and flushed it.

I had no idea where she lived or what her name was. I wondered why he didn't call her and let her know what happened. Where was he coming from? I hardly knew him. He has told a few things, and offered the painter if I needed help. He said things were not right in the warden's office. Is this why Susan isn't included in the forum meetings?

I couldn't help think about the phone call. How could I talk to his sister? Tell her and let her take the lead?

I went in the sergeant's office. We had our usual end of shift wind-up session. Talking about what we would do the next day, and small talk. Soon the midnight shift relieved me and I left to go home.

I parked my truck and ascended the steps to my home. It was just dark enough that I stumbled on the steps. When I reached for the door to unlock it, it was open. I knew I locked it when I left for work. Someone was in my house. I heard scurrying, and the sliding sound of the glass door leading to the back yard. I ran inside, and heard stumbling over the rocks in my flower garden.

"Who's there?" I yelled, reaching for the phone, and dialing 911.

"Dispatch, how may I help you?" an operator answered.

"I just arrived home, the doors were open, and I heard someone scrambled out the back door."

"I'll send the 'county boys' right out. Don't touch anything until they arrive."

While I waited, I paced the floor.

It took fifteen minutes for the two sheriff's deputies to get to my home.

They looked around, said it was a professional who knew how to pick locks. He said to place a 2 x 4 in the sliding door to prevent entry. He asked a few more questions and wrote his report.

He said to call if I found anything missing. I said I would, as the two officers left.

I sat down on the couch and said a prayer of thanks that I hadn't arrived a minute sooner. I decided to write in my journal, but when I went to the office I found papers all over the floor; my journal was gone.

Dialing the sheriff's office once again, I waited to hear the dispatch answer.

"Dispatch, how may I help you?" she said.

"This is officer Morgan again, my home was broken in this evening. The officer who came out asked me to let him know if anything is missing. The office was ransacked and my journal is missing," I said.

"Okay, I'll make a note of this and send out an officer in the morning," she said.

"That won't be necessary, I promised deputy Smith that I would report anything missing."

"I'll have him call you in the morning to discuss this." He said, "Lock your doors and remember to put the 2 x 4 in the sliding glass door. I'm sure you will be all right."

I'm sleeping with my pistol under the pillow tonight. I thought.

My thoughts reeled, wondering if the Deputy Warden had said something to the wrong person. Who has been here?

Sleep didn't come easy.

———————

I woke at eight thinking where did the night go? Reached for the phone and dialed Susan.

"Hello, Susan, I need to talk to you."

"What's it about?"

"The 'subject'"

"I'm sorry, I can't talk right now, can we meet, say at the 'Country Kitchen'? At eleven o'clock?"

"Where is it?"

"On the corner of Washtenaw and Third St."

"See you at eleven."

The phone rang just after I hung up.

"Hello?" I answered.

"This is Deputy Smith. I understand that your journal is missing, and the office was ransacked. We should come out and take finger prints…"

"No, I cleaned it up. I'm not concerned, but I wanted you to know about it." I said. "Someone needed it more than I realized."

"Alright, we'll consider it closed for now, unless you change your mind. Keep in touch." Deputy Smith said.

"Thanks I will." I said, "Good bye."

By now I knew someone felt threatened enough to want to get anything I may have written in the journal. I needed to watch my step, more now than ever before.

Randy Drake was worried. He was a part of the dope deals from the beginning. He was one of the officers responsible for the Mayberry murder. He didn't actually do the killing, but he was there. Now the warden, Mike Hale wanted to get rid of another officer. Drake didn't want anything to do with this. He had his fill of the whole fracas. He decided to talk with Joe Demming.

Joe called Drake from New Orleans, said he was on sick leave.

Drake kept Joes' phone number somewhere on his desk in the office at home.

That afternoon he went into the office, found Joes' number and dialed it.

"Hello?"

"Hey, Joe, this is Drake, how's everything? I have something to tell you. Everything here is going sour. The 'big man' wants to do in another officer, because she is a clog in the wheel, you know what I mean?"

"Sort of, yah, so what are you going to do about it.?" Joe asked Drake.

"Hey, I'm out of here, I have some money saved up, and I'm leaving for St. Louis, Mo. tomorrow morning. I thought I would warn you before you return." Randy Drake said.

"Thanks, buddy, for the warning. What's he thinking of anyway?" Joe asked.

"That's what happens, you have to keep covering up, and removing evidence. Well, we're evidence, so let this be the word for the wise. Keep out of there, for your own sake."

"Don't worry buddy, I am staying right here."

Susan and I were eating brunch when I noticed Mr. Godfry was sitting across the room with a lady, possibly his wife.

"Don't look to your right, but Mr. Godfry is over across the room with a lady." I told Susan.

She looked anyway. "We're in luck. The lady with him isn't his wife."

"Good. Well, what I need to tell you is that our 'subject' has gone to another facility. I'm not sure where though. What are we going to do now?"

"I figured this is what you wanted to talk about. I found out about it last night, he's going up north to a prison about 150 miles away. I have made arrangements for him to be sent to Campton instead, since it is closer."

"Closer? Why do you want him in Campton?"

"So you can go and see him, I still need to know what he is all about," she said.

"Why is he so important? What do you think is going on with him?"

" I can't say right now. It's involved, but I need you to continue to see him."

"This is risky. If the D.O.C. gets wind of my movements, I'm history in there. Which leads to the other reason why I called you. Someone called me and said 'YOU'RE DEAD.'"

Her face turned pale, "Who do you think it was?"

"I don't know. It was a man's voice, deep, and when I asked who it was, he hung up." I said, "And what's more, someone broke into my home last night and somebody stole my journal. I have had chest pains for quite some time now. I am ready to quit."

"You can't do that," she said.

"For you, I'll stick with it until I find what you need," I said.

"Oh, by the way," Susan went on, "Don't call the house anymore. My husband was there when you called and he wanted to know what this was all about. I guess you know that I didn't tell him anything."

Don't call her house indeed! Who does she think she is? I'm the one who is sticking my neck out; being threatened, house broken into, and getting death threats. The only reason I kept my sanity is the fact that Ralph is back and he comforts me when I am at my lowest. He still has truck trips, but they are short and nearby. This is a comfort.

―――――――――――

The next morning I went in for my appointment Dr. Betty Nolan. She weighed me first, as she knew I was dieting.

"You are doing really well. Don't loose too much too fast it's not good. How have you been feeling?"

"I have been having chest pains, I've had some scares at work, and…" I started to sob uncontrollably.

"Excuse me for a minute," she said handing me some tissue as she left the room.

A nurse entered. "I'm going to give you an E.K.G., follow me into the next room," she said.

She performed the E.K.G. and gave the results to the doctor. She had me take a stress test. The results of both tests weren't 'quite normal', so I was scheduled for a catheterization test in Star City; the hospital there had a better facility with all the modern equipment.

"I want you to take some time off, say six weeks. You need to be away from work for a while. I'm putting you on Buspar for your anxiety. Just until I get the results from the catheterization test, okay?"

"Yes, doctor. Thank You, I'm sorry for crying, I usually…"

"I know you have been holding things in too long," She said. "Here is a doctors excuse slip for the time off. Do you have sick leave coming?"

"Yes, I have 124 days saved up."

"Good, in case you will need more time off."

I can't describe how relieved I felt. It was like a weight lifted off my shoulders. No more watching, no more threats, no more blood and guts. No more traumas, no more fear…no more fear.

I drove to the prison to show the doctor's excuse slip for sick leave to administration; it said at least six weeks. They looked curiously stunned.

It doesn't matter. I need it. I'm dealing with threats, and fear for my life.

 I numbly smiled and left.

I drove home, took a pill and fell asleep. When I awoke it was eight o'clock the next morning. I jumped out of bed and stopped in my tracks; I didn't have to rush to get things done. I could just rest. And I needed a lot of it.

I poked around for the first few hours; took a shower, drank coffee out on my deck, and asked the neighbors if they noticed or heard anything the night my home was broken in to. They didn't see or hear anything. My refrigerator was empty, so I planned go to town for groceries later.

It was a nice spring day. I slipped into jeans, a cotton blouse, and tennis shoes, locked the doors, putting the 2 x 4 into place in the slider. Walked down the twelve steps to my drive where the truck was parked. It would not start. It kept coughing, and sputtering, but it wouldn't start.

I called the repair shop in town. Mr. Maynard came immediately, and tried to start it; nothing.

"It sounds to me like someone has put turpentine in your engine. Do you have any enemies?" he asked.

I held back the tears, and a choking sensation in my throat.

"Maybe, but how would they do it unless the truck was unlocked?"

"Easy, there is a tool that looks like a screwdriver with a hook on the end, all that has to be done is push it in through the grill area and pop the hood."

"How did I drive home without it stopping on me on the way home?"

"Easy, the turpentine thins the oil, then when the engine heats up, it over heats the engine and burns the valves and other parts up. When you shut the engine off, it wouldn't start again."

"Can you fix it?"

"I'll have to go back to the shop and bring the wrecker to haul it in. I can let you know after I tear down the engine to see exactly what happened. I'll call you then."

"Thanks."

I walked out to the garden, circled it, walked out back around the barn, and then back to the garden. My head was all a swirl. They are going to get me. I know I am a dead woman. Paranoia settled in.

Truck sabotaged, death threats, home broken into, my journal gone, I know too much. They think I know more than I already know. Who could it be? I knew one was a deep voiced man who said 'you're dead', but who else? There has to be more.

I was so upset I didn't notice the mechanic had been here for the truck. I was blind with fear, not knowing what to do next. I'll call Diane, she will know what to do, I thought.

"Hello, Diane you have to come over, I need to talk, right now. Please, come over, my truck has been sabotaged, and I got a call that said 'you're dead,' .."

"Wait a minute. What are you saying? Slow down," she said.

"Please come over, right now, please." I begged.

She came 10 ten minutes later.

"Okay start at the beginning," Diane said.

I didn't tell her everything; just about the death threat, the sabotage, the break-in, and how my journal is missing.

"Someone is after you? What did you do to have all this happen?"

"My job."

"You need to go to the doctor and get something more for anxiety than Buspar. You need an anti-depressant. I'll take you," she said.

I agreed.

We drove into the doctor's parking lot within the hour. I told the doctor what happened since we spoke a few days before. She wrote a prescription for Prozac, which could be taken for a short while until I felt better. She also suggested I go to a psychiatrist.

Diane was a dear. She took me to the psychiatrist the next day. He duplicated the Prozac prescription, and by that night I was in la-la land without a care in the world.

I decided that if they were going to kill me, I might as well do it myself. So I took all of the pills. I started to see geometric figures going through my mind. The figures would crunch like ice. My head felt like it was swelling, and began to pound. I panicked, and called Diane to tell her what I did.

"You little fool. I'll be right there, try to vomit," she said.

I didn't care. I was so sick I wanted to die by then.

Diane took me to the hospital where I had to drink charcoal. I almost drowned gurgling it, because they were pouring it down my throat too fast.

I don't remember what happened next. I remember being on suicide watch near the nurse's desk and telling the nurse that I would never do that again. My doctor came in and I told her the same thing. My psychiatrist came too and I told him the same thing. My headache was gone two days later and they let me go home.

I was released and told I would need someone with me for a few days. Diane said she would keep an eye on me.

I went home and told Diane she didn't have to be there, and I would be all right.

She said, "Call me, day or night, if I needed anything."

"Thanks, Diane, you are so sweet and good to me," I said, "Don't worry, I'll be alright."

Diane went home.

Dr. Nolan put me on a different anti-depressant. For the first few weeks, I didn't have a care in the world, in fact the new medicine made me feel like laughing and gave me a carefree attitude.

Ralph was indignant when he came home, because I appeared to be normal and he had to drop everything to come home. He spent the weekend and left for Louisiana the next morning. I understood his feelings. We would need the money, since I wasn't working.

Being on the meds made me feel a lot better. After a couple weeks I felt a lot better, everything seemed normal, but in the back regions of my mind I knew Susan still wanted me to go to Campton to pump Alex. She told me not to call her; so I didn't. I assume Alex is still at the prison camp about 150 miles north west of our area, because I hadn't heard from Susan.

I remembered I told Alex that I'd call his sister. I looked in my billfold to find the phone number and call her. Fortunately I still had the number.

"Hello? You don't know me but I know your brother Alex...err Andy. He wanted me to call you and let you know that he was transferred out of Jamestown Prison to another prison northwest of here," I said.

"Who are you? I heard he was gone already, about three weeks ago."

"Yes, but I promised I would call you, so .."

That sounds dumb. Why am I calling her? She knows where he is, when I don't. Maybe she can tell me something.

Maybe that's why I'm calling. You're crazy; Anne, you are really crazy for thinking it will be all right to venture into something against state working policies.

"Why don't you come over and meet me? We could go out for dinner and you can meet his cousins, nephew and nieces," she offered.

"Oh, that isn't necessary, I just ..."

"What, are you too good to meet his family?" she interrupted.

Shit! Now I'm in the middle of wanting to go out of curiosity and not going because she sounds like a gangster moll.

"When were you thinking you want me to come over?"

"This Friday night, around five. My address is 1456 Middleton Street, that's on the east-side of town."

"Oh, okay, I'll see you then," I said trying to sound enthused.

I'm going there for one thing, and one thing only, to find out what I can about Alex. Maybe I'll report it to Susan and maybe I won't. Depends on whether there is something worth reporting: like finding out if this theory about him being one of the 12 is true, or if he is in fact a rat.

Going to the psychiatrist didn't do much for me. I felt she was barking down the wrong track. To top it off she would drag on her cigarette and blow it in my face. I hated it with a passion.

Secondly, her office was a terribly long distance from my home. Her treatments were very expensive. I had an additional expense from repairing my truck, and the extra gas to travel to see the psychiatrist left me broke.

She asked the strangest questions, like if I thought I was raped when you was young, and did my mom beat me when I did something wrong. She also asked me if I thought it was a sin to dye my hair? What a waste of time.

I left my session more confused than when I went in to see her.

Chapter 36

My answering machine was blinking when I came home from the 'shrink.'

I pushed the button to play the message, "Hi, this is Susan, I need you to go to Campton as soon as possible, and report what you find."

I decided to go see Alex's sister tomorrow before going to Campton to see Alex, I'll do that Monday.

She said her name is Sarah Gump, taking her maiden name back after the divorce eight years earlier. Driving east to Allenton on Friday afternoon, I recalled our short phone conversation.

Sarah lived near the Briggs & Stratton factory in the east part of the city. I found her home fairly easily; it is the square type made during WW11, with two bedrooms, kitchen, front room and bath with a full basement. The lot was enclosed with a cyclone fence, housing a large peacock, which came to greet me.

How quaint, I thought. I rang the doorbell and a little chuwawa yipped from the other side. A young teenaged girl answered the door.

"Be quiet, Tina," she said to the tiny dog. She stepped back.

"Hi, I'm Anne," I said

"Come on in, mom's in the kitchen. She decided to have dinner here and then we will go out for a while."

I walked in and asked, "And you are?"

"Oh," she laughed, "I'm Andy's niece, Laura."

Just then a young man entered. "And this is my older brother, Jay."

I shook his hand and said, "Nice to meet you both, and you must be Sarah." Sarah came in from the kitchen to greet me.

"I was taking the roast out of the oven. Are you hungry, or would you like a drink before we eat?"

"Wine if you have it, otherwise, just tea or coffee is okay," I said.

Sarah brought me some red wine, and we sat down in the living room to talk.

"So how did you know Andy… or Alex Bartholemew as you probably know him?"

Here it comes, how much do I tell her? It's probably best to tell her just enough to open the door to ask questions and get answers from her.

"I was working at Johnstown where he was for a while."

This didn't tell her if I was there for a while or he was there for a while.

"Do you know what he is in there for?" Sarah asked.

"No, I never asked. Nor did looked it up in his files." I lied. I did read his file.

They all looked at each other for a moment, then she said, "He murdered someone. It's kind of a long story. He and his buddy were going to transport a large amount of stolen property from one place to another, in return they would get a large amount of money deposited in their bank accounts. Alex was gone for a long time. It was down in Tennessee, he would go there and bring the stuff right back. Four days passed and no one heard from him, his buddy, George, or his girlfriend, Alivia.

When Alex did finally get back to his apartment he found George in bed with Alivia. He just lost it. Alex couldn't believe George would vie for Alivias' affection. He trusted him. 'My best friend' he kept saying.

They told us he confessed to everything later. He and George took a walk to talk about the "stuff," while they were out of sight he asked him what he thought he was doing messing with his girl. George said if she didn't want to she wouldn't have. Alex took his pistol and hit George in the head, knocking him out. When George fell his head hit a rock Alex could see he was dead. He dug a hole in the vacant lot next to the apartment complex, dragged his body and buried him. The pistol was buried with George.

Alex delivered the goods, the money was deposited in his account, and he was sure he got away with it all. Then one day the police came to his door and asked him and Alivia if they had seen George. He had been missing since the day that Alex came back from Tennessee. Alivia didn't know George was missing, and began to cry. She did like George, I was told, but when Alex came back she stayed with him.

Alex told the police he had owed George some money and that he paid him, and hadn't seen him since. Alex said he thought George left the state. They searched Alex's apartment and found some blood on his clothes. Then they found out about the large deposit in his bank account after Alex returned from Tennessee. The cops questioned him until he broke down and admitted everything."

He's not one of 'us,' if this is what really happened. He is a 'rat.'

Strange, though, it is odd he didn't get rid of the bloody clothes. Why was George missed? Were the cops watching him for another reason? There are a few holes in this story.

"Wow, how do you feel about that?" I asked Sarah.

"Alex did the crime and got caught. We love him, but that's all we can do, until he gets out again," she said.

"I see. I'm sorry. He was doing fine in there. He worked on the Warden's Forum as a liaison between the prisoners and the warden."

They looked at each other, but didn't say anything.

"Well, let's go in and have our pork roast dinner. Hope you eat pork? We also have potatoes, veggies and a salad. I made a mayonnaise cake for dessert, have you ever had one?"

"Yes I have, and I like it very much." I sat my glass of half gone wine on the coffee table, and followed the three into the dining room.

While we ate, Sarah said her sister and niece would join us at the bar later: they wanted to meet me too.

I put lots of butter on my bread because I'm not a big drinker, and who knows how long they will want to stay at the bar. I was careful to watch my alcohol intake; I didn't want anyone to put anything in it either. The story Sarah told me didn't jive with what was in Alex's file at the prison. Each time they looked at each other, I wondered if they were surprised to hear a different story also; we were playing a game of cat and mouse.

The meal went fast and soon it was time to leave for the evening 'out'. I changed into a pair of black slacks and a black satin long sleeved blouse. The black Wellington boots were fine. Sarah wore something similar, and we were ready to leave.

Laura is under age for going into the bar, plus she had a date, so she stayed behind, just Jay and Sarah went with me. Sarah drove Jay and I, this was a mistake. I found out all too soon she was the kind that closed the bar.

We arrived at Mario's at eight o'clock. It was still full daylight outdoors, but when we walked through the door the darkness blinded me. I followed Sarah to the far corner booth, where we could talk and enjoy the music without the uproar of the crowd. It was so dark and smoky, that I couldn't identify anyone in the bar right away.

"So as I was telling you, Anne, Alex confessed to killing George and is in prison for life, without parole. That was the hardest part for me to overcome. We were so close, and when it happened, it took a long time for me to get on with my life. I'm a registered nurse at St. Mary Hospital, and make a good living to support my children. Jay has a job and helps out a bit but wants to find his own place. So far he lives with Laura and I. It is good to have a man around; that's one reason I haven't pushed him to find another place to live," Sarah said.

"Oh, I understand all too well. My son Claude, stayed with me for awhile before he had enough to settle on his own farm," I said.

"Do you have family?" Sarah asked.

"Yes, but tell me about your sister." I stalled her.

"Madeline is well healed. Her late husband, Frank, God rest his soul, was an engineer, and they did well. They couldn't have children, so they adopted two children, a boy, and a girl. Her son, Roger, works in California in the movie industry. You will meet her daughter, Esmarelda, tonight. She is somewhat wild, but she means well, and she sure loves her mother."

We talked for almost an hour before Madeline and her daughter, Esmareralda, joined us.

"Hi, Madeline, Esmarelda, this is Anne, a lady who knows Alex." Sara said.

The music was good; a jazz band from New Orleans, plus Earl Clugh sang and played his guitar. It was relaxing and softly played in the front of the bar away from us.

"So," Esmarelda said, "you knew my uncle, in the prison?"

"Yes for about a year or so. He wasn't on my gallery, but he did talk to me from time to time." I said.

"And he asked you to let my Aunt Sarah know where he was?"

"Yes, but I had a few things happen that kept me from calling right away. By then she already heard and found out he'd been transferred. I finally called her. She wanted to meet me and all of you, so here I am," I said.

"Oh, I'll bet he didn't tell you that I brought some 'stuff' into him; he said he had to pay a guy back for what he had done for him." She said.

"I didn't hear that, I'm not supposed to know anything about stuff like that," I lied.

"I can tell you more. He has a cronie in there that has been a mule for a long time. Every time he needs something done, this guy does it for him. He looks straight but that is a cover, and it works for him. This guy is a killer, he does it often and never gets caught," she boasted.

"You mean in the prison?"

"Yes! He is so congenial that no one ever suspects him. Everyone likes him, he is a jolly kind of person."

"You probably don't know his name, do you?"

"I can't remember, but he is a painter. He paints everywhere; the school, the chapel, even in the Wardens Office. He's like a trustee."

"Okay, I get you." I replied, "Do you take things to Alex often?"

"No, just that one time."

"Okay, that's good, because eventually you'd probably get caught."

"I know, my friend got caught doing it last year. I still deal though, do you need anything?" she lifted her bag, which was the size of a suitcase, and opened it, showing its contents. It was full of little white packages, pills, pot, and heroin.

"No thanks, I use pot once in a while, but I'm okay," I lied.

I need to ditch this gal. She is dangerous, and I don't want to get caught up in her game.

Then Jay asked me to dance. Taking the last swallow, I emptied my glass, and we went on to the dance floor.

"Is Esmarelda trying to shock you with her horror stories?" he asked.

"Ha, ha, she did have a few. She is quite the little talker, but she doesn't shock me." I said.

"The worst thing about it is that most of the stories she tells are true. Esmarelda has been very trying for my Aunt Madeline. There she goes now, hot on the trail of a new customer," he said pointing to her trying to sell weed to a guy at the bar.

I pretended not to notice. "Jay, you are a great dancer!" I said.

"I have a secret, I dance for this club to entertain women, you know, the women who aren't escorted," he said.

" No wonder, did you take lessons?" I asked.

"No, my boss, made sure I was a good dancer before he hired me. We are pretty close; he's been like a dad to me. His name is Anthony Corrazone, his nick name is 'Lefty'. He owns this fabulous nightclub called 'The Fair Heart,'" Jay told me.

I had plenty of information to tell Susan, I 'm relieved Esmarelda left, she was loose and definitely looking straight into a sad future, if she didn't get a career other than the one she had.

The music stopped, and we walked back to the table, where another drink had been ordered for me. Madeline was smiling at me, so I guessed she was my benefactor.

I looked at her and said, "Thanks."

"Tell me Anne, did my daughter bend your ear a little too much?" Madeline asked.

"Oh, no, she just told me about her connection with Alex. She seems to like him. Does she have good memories from the past about him?" I asked, trying to get more information.

"She was just a child when he went in, but she did adore him. They used to wrestle and he played with her every night when he came in from work. He would also just stopp at my home for a few minutes to visit us."

"What was his work then?"

"He was a stone mason. He built stonewalls and fireplaces. He really was an artist."

Hum, how much of this can I really believe? Did he seem this nice to me? I hadn't seen anything like this, but he was concerned that night when he shipped out. Only time would tell. In the meanwhile, my only connection was to talk to him for more information. Being on sick leave will give me more time. How did he get caught up into in a murder that led him to the prison? It doesn't jive.

"Come on back," she said, "You were day dreaming."

"I'm sorry, so what did your husband do?" I asked deflecting what was really on my mind. I knew he was an engineer of some sort, but I was trying to get her to say something to lead me to what really went on in the life of her and her brother.

"He was an engineer building bridges. My husband was on the waterfront too sometimes, building docks; you know ship docks, for big boats," Madeline said.

"Hey, that sounds like a great career he had, you can be proud of that. What a great accomplishment!"

She looked down, and didn't say anything for a minute. She said, "Yes, I was proud, but now he is in prison. He got caught up in drugs and lost everything he gained in one solitary moment. I have never gone to see him, it was hard to decide that the life between he and I was over. He will be a very old man when he gets out, if he ever does. I have a boyfriend now. He doesn't live with me, but comes and spends time with me. It fills the gap."

"Oh." I said. She had had a little too much to drink, and was talking more than I believed she would. By now I was feeling a little buzzed too, I babied two drinks and was on the third, which is dangerous for a non-drinker. I wanted this drink to be the last and I hoped we would leave soon.

Sarah was sitting there smiling at everything we said. I wanted to get more information from her too, but she clammed up and didn't say anything after we left the house.

I found it odd that Sarah told me Madeline's husband was dead. Who is telling the truth?

On the average Alex's family was okay. They treated me kindly, and made me feel welcome. By the time we left the bar, I was too drunk to drive. Sarah was nice enough to let me spend the night on her couch.

Driving home Saturday morning, gave me time to think the whole situation over. Here I am, a person on sick leave from the one of the largest prisons in the world, not knowing if I would ever go back to work there? I really wasn't sure, but it was doubtful. So many incidents had happened. I had seen more in my five years of working in there, than I had in my entire life. The psychiatrist said I have posttraumatic stress disorder. I agreed; this was too much for a farm girl to be exposed to.

I was still getting information for Susan, but couldn't figure out why. In part, my respect for her standing in the D.O.C. her decision to work with the Feds, and partly because I was very curious. Curious enough to have my life threatened though? Hopefully this was the beginning of the end. Just a visit or two then, I was done. If he didn't tell me more by then, I would quit. It felt like treading on thin ice early in the month of May.

Susan told me not to contact her by phone again, so I didn't have a chance talk to her before I planned to see Alex, at Campton prison on Monday. Andy was his legal name, I knew him first as Alexander Bartholomew. I hadn't seen him for over three months. I had a lot to say to him; the death threat, my truck engine being sabotaged, my home broken into, my journal was stolen. Without the documentation of events that happened in the last five years, it would be useless. I wouldn't have a leg to stand on, if I ever had to go to court.

When I arrived home, my horse was running along the fence, from one end of the yard to the other. She saw me drive into the yard. She was hungry. I walked right out to the barn to feed her. She thanked me by nodding her head, while chewing the hay that poked out on each side of her mouth. I filled her water trough, and went into the house.

I went to church Sunday morning, but all I could think about was the long drive to Campton the next day. I never experienced it from the other side before, visiting a prisoner. Friday night's experience, and now this, it was foreign to me, and my life style.

The pills my psychiatrist prescribed were working quite well; I hadn't had a panic attack in weeks. My attitude was much better too. I had a self-esteem that would rock the world if it knew just how bad it was before y 'break down.' It was so bad I had turned into a 'mousy Mary.' Now I am ready to face anything, except going back to work.

As I arrived at the Campton Area Facility Monday, my stomach jumped, I hadn't thought about seeing any officers I went to the academy with. I was sure I'd see at least one of them.

I asked to visit Andy Gump at the front desk. He said he would have to see if there was anyone by that name that resided there

What if Susan had it wrong, and he wasn't there yet? Several minutes passed, now it was a half-hour later. I got up and paced for a while, stopped and looked out the window at the traffic passing by across the well-groomed lawns. Susan said he was sent directly to Campton prison, from Johnstown, this wasn't true. Where had he been for the last three months?

The front desk officer finally looked up from the desk and said that this inmate had just arrived last week and to please take a seat, and I would be called when he was ready to see me.

What a relief. He is here.

A few minutes passed when an officer opened the door and looked my way. He glanced around the room and his eyes returned in my direction again.

"Anne Morgan?" the officer called my name out.

"Yes?"

"Come this way," he motioned towards the door. We need to search you before going in to visit."

He opened the door to a room that was little bigger than a closet where a female officer waited while I undressed to be searched. She checked my shoes and stopped me as I started to taking my dress off, she raised her hand and said, "That's okay, and I can check you without taking your dress off."

She shook me down, and then instructed me to put on my shoes, and said I could go through the gate and into the 'visiting room' now. I thanked her and left the room.

The gate opened. I was told to go through the gate.

"Leave your purse out for the officer to look through it," one officer said to me.

The other officer glanced through my purse, grunted and handed it back to me.

He opened the gate to the visiting room, where Andy (Alex) stood waiting. He reached for me like he was expecting me to kiss him. I froze, and stretched out my hand to shake.

"Act like you like me," he said under his breath. So I hugged him a little, and smiled big for him.

"I went to meet your family," I said.

"I heard, what do you think of them?" he asked.

"Oh, they were very good hosts. They made me feel welcome. We went out Friday evening, and I stayed overnight."

"Yes, but what do you really think of them?"

"Sarah is very nice, her son, Jay, talked to me like I knew him from before. He told me about his job at the dance club too. Laura had a date with Harold, and we went out, Sarah, Jay and I."

"What did you wear?" Alex asked me.

What? Why would this interest him? Is he being watched, and he realizes it? Probably, and most definitely, he was being watched both by the prisoners and the officers.

"I wore a black satin long sleeved blouse, and black slacks to match," I said.

"You look nice today." he said, "I like your dress."

I thanked him. *Too formal, relax, how will you get him to talk about anything, unless you make him feel comfortable? I wore my dress to make him feel more relaxed hoping he'd feel comfortable and tell me more information.*

"I haven't seen you in anything besides your uniform," he said.

"That's true. What happened to make you leave Johnstown so unexpectedly?" I asked him.

"Let's just say they wanted me to do something that was against my will, and I wasn't going to do it. I convinced the counselor to get me out of there ASAP."

So he does have a few morals, he's still a killer though.

"This is your day off isn't it?" he asked.

"Yes, but I'm on sick leave."

"What happened?"

"My life was threatened, and my truck was sabotaged."

"I knew that was going to happen. I overheard something about I, right before I was transferred."

"What did you hear?"

"Can't say. I didn't realize that I had fallen for you until I was gone. I really love you, and I want to marry you."

What! I wasn't expecting that. No wonder he wanted to kiss me. I can't marry Alex. Marrying him would be impossible. I already have a husband and family. No, I can't do this. Why would I? Even if I could marry him why would I? To get more information out of him, get answers for Susan. Not on your life. No way!

"This is sudden, isn't it? You have put me on the spot. I can't answer right away, I need time to think."

He looked at me like he was slightly disgusted with my reaction.

"Okay, think it over, but let me know as soon as you decide." he said.

"I will I promise you." I said smiling.

He put his arm round my shoulder and leaned close to my ear.

Lowering his voice he said, "You know several of the visitors are bringing in dope today. Look around you, and watch, you're good at this, just act like you're enjoying our visit and watch."

Between you and Susan I don't know who tells me to watch more often.

Looking carefully around the room, I saw three switches go down. First the lady leaned close to the prisoner, and let him fondle her. Next he was squirming around slightly. They continued talking, smiling and kissing until the visit was over. There were two other couples doing similar action.

"I see what you were trying to tell me." I said.

"If you were worked here you could bust them all," Alex said with a crooked smile. He seemed to admire me, and the work I had done.

My heart was still halfway up in my throat thinking about his proposal. I swallowed, and smiled back.

It was time to leave; I hugged him and said I'd be back next week.

I started having chest pains. I took my medicine, but his asking me to marry him was very unexpected. The pain increased, I took a few deep breaths to relax. The pain subsided, and I felt better. I slipped a relaxing gospel tape in the cassette player and sang the rest of the way home. I know I think a lot. My husband always says to ' put it in neutral.' But I never listen.

Chapter 37

"Hello?" I said into the telephone.

"How did it go?" Susan asked.

"Okay. I can tell some of it, but not on the phone."

"Brunch, same place, tomorrow at ten."

"See you there." I hung up.

She sure is testy, like she thought her phone was tapped. I wonder if she feels the same way I do? That she can't trust anyone? The warden kept her away from the meetings. I believe being a DW wasn't all that it was trumped up to being. Maybe something went on there that she was a part of, but didn't reveal it to me. I would not know until it was revealed to me and proven with facts.

The next morning I was sitting in my usual chair against the wall, waiting for Susan. I watched for her to come through the door, from my vantage point. We always sat away from the usual crowd, far enough so we could talk without being overheard. The café had a large sunroom most people avoided; this was perfect for our exchange of information.

I told her everything Alex's family told me at their home and the bar. She seemed to know about the crime that was done, but not the part about the girlfriend. She wrote Esmarelda's name down; I'm sure she wanted to carefully watch for her if she went to visit him, or any other prisoner.

When I told her Alex asked me to marry him, she became very intent, and leaned forward in her chair. Still leaning forward, she almost brought a chuckle out of me. Her chest was almost in her plate.

"Marry him! If that's what it will take for him to tell all, do it!"

"Hey, this is my life! I can't! Have you ever heard of bigamy?"

"Use his alias, Alex Bartholomew; the marriage would be illegal, and could be annulled afterward," she said.

"No, I'm not doing it. I've put my life out on a limb for you, I won't do it."

"If you don't, I will make sure you will never work in this state again."

The bitch, now she's threatening me!

"So, that's how much this means to you; you would force me to go the whole nine yards?" I asked calmly. I seethed inside.

"Yes, Anne, it means that much. I'm sorry, but I need to know."

"Well, he said the reason he was transferred was he was asked to do something he would not do, so the counselor transferred him before he was forced to do it."

"Why didn't you tell me that before?"

"I just thought about it. So many things have happened and I have gone through so much. The psychiatrist said I am suffering from posttraumatic stress disorder. Do you know what that means?"

"Sort of, something like the veterans from Vietnam?"

"That's right."

"You know it is just a new word for 'shell shock,' that's what they called it after WWII," she said.

"Right. So I have to marry this 'rat'? Use the alias, that name isn't legal is it?"

"I'll check it out, and get back with you," Susan promised.

"Before Monday, because I'm going back to see him and I want to know before I say 'yes.'"

"It'll be done. I'll call and say one word; 'No', means that it is not legal, 'Yes' means it is legal."

"Okay, Susan. Do you think your phone is tapped?"

"Yes." I thought so, just by her actions when I called.

"One more thing. Esmarelda said her dad was dead, and Madeline said he was in the pen for dope. She must have never told Esmerelda what really happened."

"Thanks, I'll check that out too."

Friday morning I came in from the barn to see I had a message on my answering machine. I pushed the button, and a female voice simply said 'no'.

The rest of the weekend went by fast, my husband was home after a long run, his last run was all the way to Oregon, then on down to Los Angles, up to Las Vegas, through Des Moines and down to Abilene, then back through Texarkana, and back through St. Louis, Chicago, then Pittsburgh and Niagara was the last stop before coming home. It had been over a month and we had a great family weekend. Ralph left early the next morning. I would miss him.

Monday came quick; my second visit with Alex was going to be more intense than the last one. I knew I would be saying yes, yet it must appear genuinely sincere to convince Alex of my intentions.

Going through the gate, I still hoped that he would spill the beans without my having to marry him.

"Hello," he kissed me.

Yuk! He smoked and I hate kissing a smoke stack. Okay, I'll play his game; I kissed him back and smiled.

"Do you have an answer?" he asked.

Let's not dispense with the preliminaries, right out with it.

"Yes, I'll marry you. Alex, that's the name I will have, Bartholomew, right?"

"Sure baby, if that's what you want." He said gently.

"Is next week too soon?" I asked.

"You are in a hurry, aren't you?"

Oooops! Don't act too eager, he may suspect something. I still don't know if I can trust him.

"Well, if we're going to do it, we might as well get it over with," I replied.

"Sure, sugar, we can do it next week."

"Will the Chaplin here do it?" I asked.

"Yes, I can arrange it for next week say Wednesday, at ten in the morning? That is the day the Chaplin can do this. Then you will have to go out and come back at the actual visiting hours."

Should I suspect something? Can I trust anything he says?

"Okay. Tell me what was it you didn't want to do when you left Johnstown?"

"I, ...well, ...okay,... I'll tell you, now that we're going to be man and wife. The warden Hale, his assistant Secretary Jones, and the head of I & I Godfry, wanted me to 'ice' you."

My heart jumped in my throat. I had no idea it was that bad.

Hold it, this could be the truth, and maybe not. Don't believe anything. Just listen and go along with it.

"But why, what was happening to want me out of the way?" I asked.

"They are bringing the dope into the prison. They have a monopoly on the amount that comes in, and want to have all the traffic wiped out so they could get all the business. You were busting their dealers as fast as they could bring it in. Lots of the other officers were too, but you didn't even give them a chance to enjoy the first joint, ...the first hit..., the first whatever they were taking."

I remembered the white packages, the light brown packages (heroine), marijuana, and the other things. Then there was the officer in 'D' block taking the dope out of the inmates cell, he ate the sandwich and had an overdose. The whole five years of being a 'good cop' flashed through my mind. Why didn't I just come in to work and do my job? Why did I want to go the whole nine yards?

"So, you are saying they put a hit on me? What else?"

"Cool it. One of the big men just came in. We can talk about it later. Just watch, and kiss me every so often."

"Which one?" I said in a lower tone.

"The big red neck, on my left near the window."

"Oh." I said and gave him a peck on the cheek.

"Watch how she gives him the dope." He said.

He hugged me so I could look over his shoulder at the transaction. It was amazing how she had it out in a fraction of a minute. The Vaseline coated package readily slipped into his rectum. He wore a pair of coveralls, which was loose, her hand was in his pants and out so fast I didn't believe it. They sat and visited for a while then she made an excuse and left. He stayed because he had another visitor waiting. This gal kissed him right away, and he gulped down something that made his throat look like a snake after swallowing a toad. The 'big red neck' was loaded, and was ready to go back to his cell to unload. The balloon full of dope would come out tomorrow.

I remembered the last guy I saw swallow a balloon. He died of an overdose before morning because his stomach acid ate through the balloon.

The big man stayed a while longer to make for a good show, then he kissed her and they said their goodbyes.

"That's how it is done," Alex said. "When I said that the painter would take care of you, I meant it. He liked you, but he was also a mule. They had something on him, so he had no choice but carry the dope to the dealers form the warden's office."

"What did they have on him?" I asked. He was telling it all. And I still wanted to hear more.

"I shouldn't tell you, but he killed someone. He got away with it, because Hale out front, said if he would 'mule' drugs for them, the murder would not show in his records."

" I guess I need to thank you for not 'icing' me; thank you. I went through a lot." I told him some of the things that happened to me, but not all. *I shivered at the memory.*

"It's time to go, I'll see you Wednesday, next week at ten o'clock." I said.

He squeezed my hand and we smiled at each other lovingly.

I felt I needed someone to witness what DW Lorenzo and I talked about. By now she was filled to the brim with information., and I had more to give her. I was so close to what I felt she needed; yet I wanted my hubby who was out of town, my daughter or someone to be there. I still didn't trust her or Alex. I arranged to have my daughter Angel come with me to meet Susan. We arrived early and had breakfast finished by the time Susan arrived. I introduced her to Angel; she paused for an instant, then she said, "How very nice to meet you."

Angel shook Susan's hand saying, "You two go ahead and talk, I'm writing a thesis for college and will only be here until I have to leave for class."

Angel bent her head in a book and pretended to be studying.

"Let's get right to the facts. You asked me to go ahead and marry this joker, since he hasn't told me enough. Right?"

"Right."

Angel kicked my knee under the table, to let me know she had the tape player on.

"So, Andy Gump has arranged to have the prison Chaplin perform the ceremony. He has also agreed to use his alias, Alexander Bartholomew, for my sake, I said I liked it better. So far all he said that he was asked to 'ice' me, for the purpose to stop me from finding all the dope brought into the prison. The dope dealers considered me a 'thorn' in their side, but I wasn't budging, or shall I say, 'playing ball'. He also said the corruption was all the way up to the warden. They were involved in officer Yvonne Mayberry's death, and said they didn't want to do a sloppy job again, when killing me. The only thing that saved them during Mayberry's death was the fact that the Robinson who took the rap was drunk and didn't know how the bloody clothes got in his cell. He had nothing to lose that he couldn't be in there any longer than the three life sentences he was serving already."

"What, are you saying?" Susan asked, with her eyes bulging.

"I'm telling you what he told me. Mayberry's killer was in for three life sentences and he had nothing to lose by confessing to her murder, and taking on a fourth life sentence.

Also, when Andy/ Alex refused to kill me they said they would make it rough for him, so he agreed to do it. When he left the office, he leaned against the wall and heard them say they had to get rid of him too, and probably would use 'the painter.'" I said.

"Should I ask you if there is anything else?" she asked me.

"Yes there is, but I need to know for sure, who the big man is. I'll find out next week, when I go to my 'wedding.'"

"Okay, listen to me. You have told me enough, you have never met me; you have never talked to me. Someone else will contact you from now on. Do not call me; I'm changing my phone number. I will deny it if you say we were involved in this research," she said sternly.

Angel looked at her watch and said, "Woops, got to go", and slapped everything into her briefcase under the table, "Nice to meet you," she said to Susan. She gave me a quick hug and left.

Susan sounded like she was scared stiff. I was not sure what to expect next, so I made small talk before we parted. I didn't see her again until we were in court.

_____

Sleep didn't come easy. My mind had everything running through it.

I knew it was a good decision to tape record the final conversation with Susan. I was concerned for my daughter Angel. Could she be in danger?

I also thought about Alex, our wedding, and what he may tell me after the wedding. Could I finally trust him? He told me more than I believed he would.

I wondered about who would contact me, would I go along with the new contact?

I tossed and turned. Sleep wouldn't come. I got back up and took a sleeping pill.

It all started with a few people getting together at a beautiful resort overlooking a small private lake surrounded by birch and popular trees. It was winter; and all the leaves were off the trees, but there was still no snow on the ground. The grass was green in some spots. The home set in a hill. The wide spread of windows enabled a panoramic view from both stories.

Everyone was upstairs, having a drink. Mine was rum and coke. Suddenly I began to feel ill, I went for the bathroom. "Where is the bathroom?" I asked my hostess, vaguely remembering who she was. She said, "Across the hall to your left."

A younger, blond, skinny girl, Shelia Jones said, "Here let me help you."

I grabbed her arm because I was falling; she let me slide down the wall to the floor. I recognized her to be the warden's secretary, Shelia Jones. I saw her reach for a square package and pull out a white pill as I slid to the floor passing out. Everything went black.

I woke up in the middle of a great room surrounded by a crowd of people I didn't recognize. I described Shelia Jones giving me a white pill, when one of the ladies said,

"She's my sister." The words echoed in my head. 'Sister, sister, sister.'

"Oh, I didn't realize that." I said. '...*that, that, that.*' The word echoed.

"You must have had the same spell that you had at work twice before."

What? Who is this lady? How does she know I passed out at work? Twice did she say? I don't remember.... Don't rememb..."

"Well no, I don't think so..... I was dizzy, but never a black out," I said slowly.

"Are you sure?"

I looked at her eyes; the look she gave was not friendly. People began coming up from downstairs. I didn't realize so many people were present. Susan Lorenzo was there, I almost didn't recognize her, her hair was long and turned under, and she had lost over 40 pounds, her curly haired friend, the librarian Vivian Green, and two more 'ladies.' All four ladies were smiling, and whispering to each other, but I couldn't hear them. My mind was racing. What was going on?

I looked around the room. Everyone was there. We met at a large resort mansion home. Everyone was there from the prison administration staff, officers, and civilian workers.

"KILL ME" the note said when I unfolded it. The man had come in from hunting. I thought he was going to shoot me, he kept lowering the rifle at me, my eye-sight was blurred. Floating, I ducked behind the bed, that's when he handed me the rifle and the 'kill me' note.

It was then that I realized that it wasn't a rifle after all; it was a shotgun, with a 20 round clip like the mini-14 rifle.

That's crazy.

I finally realized who the hostess was. Sgt. Jesse Landry. The one that was so friendly to the prisoners and transferred. I had written her up when I first started working for the state. She was promoted and transferred to a medium security prison after I wrote her up. I hadn't even finished my drink, and they were on their fourth. It was obvious why I felt like I did, someone had put something in my drink.

I was accompanied into an adjoining room to talk to three men about my 'previous blackouts.' I looked down at my dress, and saw it was dirty from when I fell.

One of the three men was my partner from the first day in the block; Andrew James, I knew I could trust him.

Mr. Reginald Warner, my old school principal, stepped into the room. He looked very stern and none too friendly, which surprised me; he was always friendly and usually had something nice to say. He looked me up and down, turned and left the room.

I went after him and called out. "Mr. Warner?"

"Yes?"

'I have always liked you," I said.

He smiled and said, "Thank you, my dear."

I woke up, shaking my head from side to side. What a strange dream. Mr. Warner was my Principal at High School in the mid seventies. Why was I dreaming about him? I looked at the clock; it was 3:15 am. It was the morning before my wedding to Alex.

Chapter 38

Morning came. I awoke to the sound of rain falling against the window of my bedroom.

My husband knew I had to go somewhere, but I had not told him about this part of my "research'. It was enough for Angel to get involved. She had made me promise to not go, but I knew I had to.

I dressed in a nice suit with a matching hat. The suit was teal blue, rather feminine gored tight waist with a ruffled edge design. I should look the part.

I arrived at the Campton Prison at 9:45, walked in and found that the Chaplin was waiting. Soon Alex was brought up from his lock, and we were sent into the room next to the reception desk. The room was seldom used; it smelled like new varnish and floor wax.

The Chaplin said a few words before asking, "Alexander, do you take this woman to be your wedded wife?"

"I do," he said with a grin.

Then he looked at me and said, "Anne, do you take this man to be your wedded husband?"

"I do." I said.

"Now I pronounce you man and wife. You may kiss the bride."

That was it. I was married to an inmate. I sure hope I know what I'm doing.

" What will you do when you go back inside?" I asked Alex.

"Just sit around and wait to see you again at one. And you?"

"I'll go downtown to the mall to window shop."

"You won't eat anything, will you?"

"No, why?"

"Because, I thought we would get a lunch cake out of the machine and feed each other, like they do at normal wedding ceremonies."

"Oh, good idea," I said.

"Ok. I'll see you later. We'll talk then."

"Okay, we'll talk then," I said turning to leave.

I left the facility, knowing I would have to come back to get the other side of the story.

I drove downtown, browsed in the mall, then went into the Main Street Café, had lunch, trying to kill time until one o'clock. Soon the two hours passed, it was time to return to the prison.

At one o'clock, I was back at the prison, waiting to be called to the visiting room.

"Ms. Morgan you may come in now," an officer said.

"Hello, my wife," Alex said bending to kiss me.

This is the last day. I'm never coming again. If I can just get through this, and get him to tell me the rest of his story. I'll be out of here for good. Then it's Good Bye, Sayonara, Adieu, Aufvedersien, Haste la vista, I'm out of here.

"Let's sit over here by the window," Alex said. "Now that we're married, we can go out in the courtyard too."

It stopped raining, and the sun dried off the benches, so I said we should sit outside. At least the air would be fresher than inside.

"It is a beautiful day, isn't it?" I said making small talk.

"Yes, if I wasn't in here," he said in a sad tone.

"Let's be positive. Your sister, Sarah, said you were a stone mason before, do you think you will go back to that line of work when you get out?" I asked.

"I haven't really thought about it. You know, I should; something tells me you will bring me good luck."

"For your sake, I hope so." I said. "She said that you were an artist in your work. I could tell she is proud of the things that you created before."

"I guess so. She is partial though. Look, there's the red neck, Jerome M. Dillon, for his weekly drop. Let's go in and sit near him, okay?"

"Sure. That will be fine."

This may be the chance I need. Don't look too anxious, just act like a curious new bride. Listen, watch and ask when you deem it necessary.

We sat next to the window, behind Jerome Dillon, the red neck. His girlfriend was seated against the window, with Bill next to her. Alex sat next to the window, and I slid beside him.

"Hey bro', this is my girlfriend, Shelia Jones, she comes all the way over from Tennessee, each week to see me. She fly's over and back the same day," Jerome said.

"Nice to meet you, this is my wife, Anne. We were just married this morning," Alex said.

"How do you do?" I said to Shelia and Jerome.

Jerome looked me over and said, "She will be a good one for us, won't she bro?"

"Yah, she probably could be, we'll talk about it."

Oh no I won't. I'm out of here after today. Just talk to me honey, give me everything you know.

"Hey, how's about we turn our chairs around so we can talk together?" the brute said.

They both turned around facing us. I noticed he was wearing a large pair of bib overhauls. I could see his shorts and hairy body.

Shelia was a slightly over-weight woman, with medium brown hair, forty-'ish' white woman. She was dressed well I thought; wearing a silky dress.

The 'red neck' was grinning and looking from me to Andy and back.

"This is a watch and see lesson, you notice Shelia's pockets don't have a bottom in them. It is easy for her to go through the bottom of her pocket, straight to her vagina. She reaches for the goods, and when we hug she slips them into my pants, the open bib overalls, easy for me to wiggle it up my Vaseline coated rectum."

The guys apparently had talked ahead of time. Alex and Jerome, the redneck, planned before hand to show me the ropes, so I could start helping to carry in drugs. For a hot second I was indignant, and then I knew.

I pretended to play dumb and listen.

"I didn't hear your name, sir. I can't say 'hey you.'"

"It's Jerome M. Dillon. Sheila and I are going to get married soon too."

"How very nice for you both." I said.

"Hey, homie, she's educated, and mannerly too," Jerome said to Alex.

"Thank you."

"How do you find it so easy each week?" I asked.

Shelia and Jerome looked at each other, and she said, "I get it from a supplier, who flies it in from Columbia. He comes every two months, but I can't bring it all in at once, so I bring as much as possible every week."

"You're kidding me, aren't you?" I smiled.

"She's green, isn't she? No honey, we're telling you the truth. He's coming again soon, too, isn't he, Shelia?"

"Yah, Lorenzo will be in sometime next week, I'm not sure. He'll call me. Jerome has a cousin at the prison where you work. I go there too. It has worked out better than our original plan in the food delivered. Things kind of got hot there, so the plan changed after a near scare," Shelia said.

Holy shit! Lorenzo? As in Susan Lorenzo, the DW I have been contacting every time I had a report for her? Is this a coincidence or just a common name?

Shelia must have felt safe, thinking that I didn't recognize the name, or was indifferent to who brought it in. I carried on like every thing was 'kosher' the big thing was to catch the supplier, not the mules.

"Now that we have you, Anne, we can bring in twice as much and make that much more money."

I smiled and nodded my head.

"I'll be here next Monday. If you need me, before hand, let Alex know, and he can contact me." I said.

"Just give Shelia here a number where you can be reached," Jerome said.

"Here it is, 935-555-1221."

"Got it, thanks. You'll be hearing from me." She smiled.

Shelia had passed her package. She made little talk, and after a few minutes she said her good-byes. Andy needed a cigarette pretty bad, and was squirming some because of it.

Was he carrying a package out to general population? I wondered? When did I take my eyes off Shelia long enough for her to get some to Alex? Only time will tell. Alex did look surprised when she said she took the dope into Johnstown. If the warden is the main man at that site, Alex possibly didn't know about the supplier. It's out of my hands; he could act on whatever he is all about. Thank God I won't be here. I have heard enough to back off after I relate the information to my next contact, the FBI man. Whoever that may be, I'll know all in due time.

209

Chapter 39

There was a message on my answering machine when I arrived home that afternoon.

A note on the table said, 'I will be gone until Friday. He signed it hugs and kisses, Ralph.'

A soft tenor-like man's voice said, "Call me, I'm your new contact." 937-555-3913."

I dialed the number, "Hi, you asked me to call?"

"Yes, I would like to take you for a walk in the nature park in Castlebrook tomorrow, at ten o'clock. It is a good place for us to have privacy."

"How will I know you?" I asked.

"Look for a man in a trench coat, I'll be waiting at the entrance gate."

"Okay, I'll see you then."

"I'll be waiting at the entrance gate."

I have no idea who this man is, nor do I know what he looks like. How do I know I can trust him? I felt very uneasy the rest of the day.

Okay.

So I go, and they find my body six years later. The news states that the body is badly decayed, only the dental reports, after an extensive research, reveals who the victim is. They are puzzled why she was there, while her husband was out of town. The news went on to say that there was speculation that she had a lover, and that it could have went awry.

Boy, let your imagination flow, this is it. You will give the info to him and it will be over. Not to worry.

After all you have gone through already, this will be a snap! Snap? Of my neck?

Ugh! Quit worrying.

Just get it over with.

I took a sleeping pill, and went to bed.

No nightmares tonight, no, I will sleep like a baby and be fresh as a daisy in the morning.

I woke with the birds chirping, and the sun in my face. I leaped from bed. It was eight thirty. I had just one hour to get ready before I met this mystery FBI manta the nature park in Castlebrook.

A man stood at the gate waiting for me as I drove into the parking lot at precisely at ten o'clock. He was wearing a tan trench coat, and a gray suit.

Not exactly the kind of clothing one would wear for a hike. Who was he? FBI? Deputy Warden?

He reached my side and said lowly, "Don't shake my hand, just reach over and hug me."

I smiled for onlookers, and hugged him.

What are you, out of your mind? I asked myself.

He introduced himself as a friend of a friend. "I'm DW Susan Lorenzo's friend, so to speak."

"Tell me more," I inquired.

"She is someone you have been talking to for two years on a particular subject. We are studying the prison for drug trafficking, as well as conditions in the prison. Also the deaths of two officers, as we have been watching for sometime now. There are 12 of us in Johnstown, six are prisoners, and six are officers. You have been put through more than most. Some of the officers left after six months; you stuck it out the longest. I believe you have something to tell me today that will conclude your part of this study."

How well put, I thought.

So now I tell everything I know. You 'ice' me and no one sees me again.

At least I know he is a Fed. Well, that's what Susan told me. She said if I ever tried to tell anyone this in a court of law she would deny it. I could understand. She had to cover her back. The man was looking at me for a response.

"I won't repeat the things I found out about the warden, his assistant, and the guy in internal investigations, so far it's hearsay. Other than that, I do believe Hale, Malinski and Godfry, are involved in the death of Officer Mayberry. I was informed by a prisoner, who I trust, he never asked me to do anything, nor indicated it," I said.

I gave him the list of other officers I suspected were involved. This was his job, to check them out.

"You have good insight for saying that," he said.

"Yesterday, I received information that no doubt will surprise you. You may have to follow up on some of it to find out for yourself if, in fact, this is the lead you've been waiting for."

Someone was coming our way. He paused and said, "Let's sit on the bench," he took my hand so it would appear that we were lovers, just a clandestine moment in the park.

Once we were seated, he took both my hands in his, and held them.

"Okay, look into my eyes turning my way a little, you were saying?" he said.

The smug self-assurance showed through, ah, to be like him. He hasn't even offered a name. Who the hell was he? What's your name fella? Do show me a certain amount of respect. What am I stupid or what? Maybe.

"What do I call you anyway?" I blurted out.

"It really does not matter, but for the record I'm Tom O'Brien."

Probably a fake name, I thought.

"Okay, Tom, dope is being flown in every two months from Columbia to Tennessee, to Campton. The outside mule is Shelia Jones; she has a place in Tennessee, and stays here with her cousin when she is in town. She supplies both Campton and Jamestown prisons. Her supplier, Lorenzo, flies in every so often from Columbia to Chattanooga, Tennessee with the goods. He is going to arrive sometime next week."

"Are you sure?" he asked.

"I swear it, that's what she said."

I could see his wheels turning; his mind was in overdrive.

He pulled a pipe from his jacket, packed it, lit it and said, "You did well. You will be hearing from us soon."

"So my job is complete. Right?"

"Yes, and thank you. We'll take the tap off your phone now. Feel free to relax and go on with your life as if nothing ever happened."

"I didn't realize that there was a tap on my phone," I said surprised.

"We're sure you didn't. By the way you talked we knew, yet you never revealed yourself to anyone." He paused, and then added, "Thanks again and like I said, you will be hearing from us."

The weight on my mind was lifted, but I knew until all the guilty parties were behind bars, I was still more than just a little nervous. The truth is the knot in my stomach, the clutching grip on my heart would take more than a day to subside, and be completely gone.

Chapter 40

"There's been a change of plans. My man is coming in to Chattanooga, Tennessee. You will pick up his packages, and fly into Campton as usual. You will not have to take the long flight to Columbia this time."

"Got it, boss man," North said to Hale.

"The money will be with the packages, that is your cut." Mike Hale said.

"Thanks. I'll be waiting on the field in Chattanooga." North said.

He was brief and to the point. North hung up, leaving Hale looking at the dead phone.

_____

O'Brien, who's real name was Chuck Brimstone left the nature park and headed east towards his office. He hated to lie to her, about his name, but it was necessary.

He had a job to do, and it must start immediately in order to get a few good men around by the next day and arrange for enough time to get to Chattanooga to have cover at each airport.

He called the home office, and told his boss everything, including the information he found about this morning, and concluded by telling him what he needed.

"There are three airports, the main one and two secondary ones farther out in the country. I will need enough personnel to cover all three."

"Right, so how many will it take to cover this?" asked his boss Raymond Bellamy, the regional Director.

"At least 15 per, total forty-five good men and women."

"Got it, you will need warrants, dogs, and the proper costumes, uniforms, etc. I'll take care of everything."

There are three airports in and around Chattanooga. The head office in Chattanooga sent 18 good agents. Men who were trained to cover as mechanics, tellers, repair men, guards at the gates, blind persons with seeing eye dogs. A few good women too, to look like partners, etc.

Chuck Brimstone and Raymond Bellamy planed to join the 18 agents in Chattanooga, to see fruition in their work in New York.

Seven would be assigned to each airport. The day shift would have a crew of four and the nights three.

In the past a big drop would use a small strip to land a single engine plane, which could land, make the drop, and fly out just as quickly. This part of the cover would take an expert air trafficker, to say the least. In all probability, one of the smaller airports would be the target. Still, each airport should be covered, to make absolutely sure to catch the imported dope smuggler.

Raymond Bellamy called a retired agent who lived near Chattanooga. Charlie Grimes had retired as an agent, and started a Dude Ranch, just for a retired leisure atmosphere.

"Hi, Charlie, How's everything? This is Ray."

"Ray, old buddy, what's up?" Charlie said.

"Does there have to be something up?" Ray chided.

"Well, we did say there was a possibility that we would never contact each other unless it was necessary. Remember that?" Charlie asked.

"Yes I do. The truth is I need to house around 20 agents for a few days. Do you have the room?"

"Must be something hot. Sure, consider it done." Charlie said.

Within a few hours the team was landed in Chattanooga. They arrived at all three airports, in their dude ranchers attire, and separate groups. They arranged to meet at a nearby horse ranch owned by Charlie Grimes, a retired agent.

This horse farm was huge, and in season it's occupancy 65 residents, who usually were weekend cowboys or on sabbatical for a week or two. The ranch was an ideal spot to meet, stay and rotate the twelve-hour shifts at each airport, for each day of the coming week. The plan was to take each day until Lorenzo made his appearance.

Headquarters hand picked the best of the best, coordinated pairs to appear as man and wife, some came single, but all were dressed in western attire when they landed, acting like dude cowboys on vacation.

It was easy to guise as a blind man when 'Lassie' arrived with a sweet newly wed couple to spend the week at the 'Dude Ranch'. Lassie was a trained yellow retriever, a dog that could smell dope through a foot of cement.

The 'blind man' dressed differently, and was a different man each day.

The women were posing as tellers, and clerks, one was a guard. The men were loading luggage, mechanics, and guards also. Gate personnel were a mix of both.

Monday came and went without anything suspicious.

When Tuesday came, one person came off the airplane, with a carry on box large enough it deemed examining. The golden retriever didn't growl, but the box was questionable. When it was opened, there was a collection of rocks gathered from the ecologist's trip to the mountains in South America. This was close, but a false alarm.

Wednesday went without event also.

Thursday around ten o'clock, a man in a wheel chair flew in from Columbia. He slid to one side of his chair, and looked exhausted from the trip. The man had white hair and a white mustache, and wore a black top hat and a black coat to match. An attendant was pushing him slowly to the baggage claim area. She was carrying his tote bag for him.

George, an agent in the baggage department was on the lookout for unusual baggage and boxes. He was suspicious when he lifted a suitcase; it weighed over 50 pounds, which is unusually heavy. He also found cardboard box triple tied with meat wrapping string that looked suspicious. It measured eighteen inches long, ten inches wide and eight inches deep.

George reached for his radio and talked lowly to Chuck.

"There's a luggage bag that weighs about 50 pounds, and a package that weighs around 30. The package is wrapped in a butcher-shop paper and white string," George said.

"Okay, we'll be watching to see who picks each one of the packages up," Chuck said, "Henry, bring 'Goldie' up near the baggage belt, near the opening where the luggage and boxes come from the back. If she growls, lift your hat and scratch your head."

Chuck was sitting near the baggage claim area, reading a newspaper, and smoking his pipe. The baggage came out on the circular moving belt.

Black, brown, green, there's a Marlboro red bag, too light, the 'cover,' Frank thought to himself, then set it back saying 'wrong one' smiling. The outside luggage man buzzed in the wire to watch for the huge thirty-pound case, he was intent on getting it.

The team of four were ready; Chuck, sitting in one of the chairs near the wall, the luggage man, George, watching and ready to come through the door between the back and front of the luggage claim, Henry, the blind man,

When the elevator opened, and the attendant wheeled the old out, followed by another woman and man, who were using walkers.

 The old man in the wheel chair said, " Thank you for your help," to the attendant, "my daughter will be along soon to help me."

Chuck watched for Shelia. He had a description of her and was sure he would recognize her.

The old man's 'daughter' walked up to him, and reached down to hug him. When she straightened up and turned her head, Chuck recognized it was Shelia Jones!

He talked into the wire, "They're here, get ready and wait for the pick-up," Chuck said into his radio. Shelia reached first for the wrapped cardboard box, and said, "Daddy is this your box?"

The old man nodded and said, "My bag, don't forget my bag. It's the one with the green yarn on the handle, that one, the big black one," he said in an unsteady voice.

Chuck had moved closer pretending to look for his luggage. He reached over to help her, and said, "Here let me help you." he smiled, "Is this the one?"

"Yes, but I can get it." Shelia said as she grabbed it off the belt.

Chuck slapped the cuffs on her wrist immediately.

She screamed, attempting to warn Lorenzo.

The old man in the wheel chair jumped up and ran toward the door. Three agents converged on him. He quickly escaped their approach, going through the door and across the street into the parking garage.

Surprisingly he could run faster than most. He sprinted like a man who was in training for a track meet. Three agents, the guard, the blind man and the baggage man ran after him.

The old man was running like he wasn't a day over forty-five years old. The agents converged on him, tackling him to the ground.

His mustache had fallen off; part of the makeup also had fallen off. An agent removed his fake wig, revealing a much younger man. Lorenzo had been captured.

Two guards were watching near the runway, noticing a single engine Pfeiffer running with the pilot standing nearby.

When the 'guards' were sure Lorenzo was in custody, they approached the pilot.

North seen them coming and scrambled to get into the cockpit. His hand was on the edge of the cockpit with one leg raised to jump in.

Bellamy and Williams, approached the plane, running as Bellamy grabbed Bob North just as he was nearly in the cockpit.

North fell to the ground with Bellamy under him. Williams grabbed North and cuffed him. He was taken in for questioning.

Chapter 41

Marlow Malinski, the warden's secretary, had a degree in criminal justice, yet she lacked the confidence a career woman should have. She used her good looks and sexy body to get her where she wanted to go. The position she held today she believed; earn it after all didn't she? Being a nymphomaniac made her career advancements easier.

Marlow worked with the Department of Corrections for a long time, working in the administration department, at first doing filing in the front office. She made it known to each male boss she had, just how far she would go to advance. After all, she would enjoy every ounce of the favors she bestowed on them.

Now she was almost to the top. She was the warden's secretary. This covered a various amount of duties including attending many functions his wife was too 'ill' to go to. His wife suffered from heart disease. Logically it was all right for Mike to take his secretary. She was more acceptable then someone else.

If Mike Hale would just allow a helper, she could be the patsy.

Marlow explained to her boss she needed an assistant. Marlow couldn't do everything that was expected of her. There were just too many responsibilities. So Mike allowed an office girl for her.

His forehead furrowed, and he walked into his office to get away from her nagging. She was another mistake he had made. But, she was there for him, doing things above and beyond the call of duty.

Marlow was exactly where she wanted to be. She was content for more than one reason. Her pay was equivalent to the Captain's, $52,000.00 annually. She had an assistant to do the dirty work.

Mary, her assistant came to work 1987 about six months after 'the problem' in the spring.

If Mayberry, the stupid bitch, hadn't discovered their dirty meetings, their romantic clichés, their exchange of bodily secretions, male and female alike, there wouldn't have been a problem.

Many of the administration were in on it, enjoying every moment of the orgies.

If anything ever went wrong, she was ready to point fingers.

The phone in the den of warden Mike Hales' home rang.

"Hello, this is Mike," he said into the phone.

"Meet me right away at the corner of Main, and Connate. It's urgent," the director of the Department of Corrections Malcolm Fairchild said.

"I'll be there in ten minutes." Mike said hanging up the phone.

The townhouse, where he spent time near the job and his secretary, Marlow, was a few minutes away. The director never contacted him unless it was absolutely necessary. Mike knew the he had a lot to lose if any of this leaked to him. Mike would likely be the fall guy. Mike knew exactly what he would have to do in that instance.

He pulled up behind the Director's car. He got out of his car and climbed into the passenger seat of the directors' car.

"What took you so long?" Malcolm Fairchild, snarled at Hale.

"Traffic," Mike gave a sheepish grin.

"All hell has broken loose, Mike. We have to lay low for a while until it subsides."

"What are you talking about?" Mike asked.

"Lorenzo has been caught!" Malcolm almost shouted it. "They've arrested your pilot North, too. It's just a matter of time and they will be knocking on your door."

"That damn fool, how did it happen? How did they catch North too?"

"Probably that Shelia slipped and talked to someone. I don't know." He went on, "I can tell you this, my name better not be attached to anything that has been done here. You know the consequences… I don't need to say any more. The word is no squealing, or you will bleed like a stuck pig."

"Don't worry, don't worry. I'll take care of it. No one will ever know. Everything will be taken care of."

"Everything had better be taken care of. I don't know you. You're the warden, that's all I know. You hear, I don't know you, or any of your off duty excursions."

The Director raised his hand, " I'm done with this conversation, be gone."

Chapter 42

Mike Hale knew Lorenzo was arrested. The sordid tale was released on the news. Malcolm Fairchild was right. The FBI Agents talked about those responsible, just as though they already knew the culprits involved in the drug bust.

After his conversation with the director Malcolm Fairchild, Mike knew he couldn't break. He couldn't tell anything. He was innocent, he would tell his accusers. He must keep his mouth shut. He wasn't ready to be a stuck hog.

Mike Hale didn't sleep well that night. He worked reasoning out, how he would get away with the things he had done. The words were repeated over and over in his thoughts. Sleep didn't come until he was satisfied with his plan.

The next morning in the wardens' office, Mike paced back and forth in his office. His secretary, who couldn't help but notice, came in to see what was happening.

"Mike, what's wrong?" asked Marlow. She closed the door behind her, and ran to his open arms. He looked so dejected.

"Our supplier has been caught. You know what will happen next? It is just a matter of time before we will be caught too. I am an old man. Do you realize, Marlow, how old I'll be when I get out? This will kill my wife, with her weak heart. Marlow, I will take good care of you and make sure you have everything you need in there, but you will have to be the one to confess."

He had his arms around her, holding her close; her head was resting on his shoulder. He held a smirk of contentment.

Marlow was crying, she patted his back and said, "It will be alright, I will tell them that Lt. Wainwright was the one who killed officer Mayberry, since his suicide no one will know the difference. I just kept the information to myself, because of the fear of what would happen to me.

"As far as the dope, I can say you didn't know anything about how it got into the prison, nor will I tell how the 'boys' got it through, or the 'boys' on the warden's forum part. But you must remember what you promised, or I will spill the beans, remember I have proof and it's in a safe place." Marlow said.

"I know, I know, you little vixen. We've had a great run for our money. I will be eternally grateful for your devotion." His face held an expression that showed relief, and satisfaction as well. He held her closer, and lifted her face for a sweet kiss.

The intercom buzzed, Mary, Marlow's assistant, was on the other end, "Excuse me Mr. Hale, a man is here to see you, by the name of Clarence Wright from the Federal Bureau of Investigation."

They both leapt apart, straightening their clothes.

"Send him in please will you Mary?" Marlow attempted to make her leave. "Marlow, stay here and take notes," Mike said.

Clarence Wright walked in through the opened door. He stood six foot two inches, clad in a gray suit, and trench coat to match. He reached out his hand and said, "Hello, I am Clarence Wright, with the FBI," he said flashing his ID card.

"What can I do for you, Mr. Wright?" the warden Mike Hale said.

"We have been investigating the prison for quite some time, because of the deaths of two officers, and suspected dope dealing.

My informants have lead me to your office, so at this time I and my assistant who is waiting out in the front office will be placing you and your Secretary under arrest. I have these warrants here."

"Did you say three?" Hale's heart leapt, they must know about the Director of D.O.C., Malcolm Fairchild.

"Three? No, I said these. These warrants."

"I, …" the warden was interrupted.

"That won't be necessary," Marlow said. "I am the guilty one."

She hung her head slightly and confessed to everything, telling exactly how it all happened. She and the warden, Mike Hale had rehearsed exactly what she should say.

"We were having our usual orgy, four of us. We would meet in the room adjacent to the Prison School. There was a desk there where we put the lines of coke out to snort. Coke enhances the exotic sex experience."

She didn't wait for a reply, "We had a mattress there where the action took place, and I was doing two of the guys when officer Mayberry came in. She said she was going to tell. I yelled, "kill the bitch," and Lt. Wainwright hit her over the head with his radio. She screamed. It was then he took his belt off and strangled her. The two other officers Randy Drake and Joe Demming, raped her dead body. They left the state, and we don't know where they are. Lt. Wainwright later shot himself."

"We know where they are, they both are in our custody at this moment," said FBI agent Wright. He looked at Warden Hale and continued saying, "You know we will have to take you in for questioning also, to help clarify Marlow's statement."

"Yes, I understand, but I didn't know anything about this. I didn't have anything to do with any of this." He stuck to this to the bitter end. Even the day in court he calmly said, "I didn't know anything about what was taking place in my prison."

Chapter 43

I went to one of Bloomington's most famous and capable lawyers in the area, Smith, Smith and Jones. I told Mr. Jones everything that had happened; the things I was asked to do, the death threats, truck sabotaged, my journal being stolen, the break-in at my home, everything; except the part about my cooperation with the FBI. I elaborated on my break down and the meds I was taking to survive the posttraumatic stress I had received from work experience. He said I had a case to sue the state for liability.

He reached to the recording machine and punched the 'record button.'

"This is what I will say in court: 'My client was raised in the country, a quiet place where the most exciting thing that ever happened was the annual county fair, and a weekly trip to church on Sunday. She grew up to be honest and innocent, seriously naive of what the world was all about. Some would say she was gullible. But it was just plain ignorance. She never realized how the other side of life was with no street knowledge.

My client's experience has left her cold, and feeling labeled a 'whistle blower.'

The worst part of the entire situation was that the very person, who wished to fire her, is the one who should be fired.

If you were asked to do something by your superiors while still fresh in your job your natural instinct would be to want to. She did not know, and wasn't totally aware it was not a part of her duties. But, as events took place she began to wonder whether she should be doing what she was asked.

She finally had to make a grave decision, which could affect her job and families welfare. She had to make a judgment call.

Will she be sorry for telling on my superiors? No.

What is more important? She knew what was right for the majority of people. Justice must be done. That is when she 'blew the whistle.' That was her final judgment call.'

I took in a deep breath.

"What you just said sums it up just exactly how I felt, what I experienced, and why I did it. And finally, why I feel the state is responsible for my post-traumatic stress, " I said to my attorney, Mr. Jones.

"Don't worry, we'll take care of you," said Mr. Jones. He patted my back as I left his office. "I'll call you when we have your hearing scheduled."

"Thanks, Mr. Jones."

"Hello?" I answered the phone.

"Hello, this is SGT. Rogers. I heard that you will be suing the state, can we talk?"

Word gets around fast. I thought

"Sure, I'd talk to you anytime; my respect for you is tops," I said.

"You need to hear my story, Anne, I was asked to watch Officer Brown, that's when I went into 'A' block just before you came to the block to work for me. As a result of reporting what I found, I was told to back off. I refused, and the next thing you know, my truck was sabotaged," Sgt. Rogers said.

"So was mine! I received a phone call saying, 'YOU'RE DEAD!' Our experiences are so parallel" I exclaimed.

"You went through a lot, didn't you?"

"Yes, but it's all over now." I said, feeling relief.

"I just wanted you to know you were a great 'cop.' And if you need me at the trial, I'll be there. In fact I'll be there anyway to give you moral support," Rogers said.

227

My hearing was brief.

Susan Lorenzo, and the man from I&I, Godfry, sat together on one side of the room, while my daughter, Angel, Sgt. Rogers, Dan Romley, a good officer and close friend, who was in the gun squad during the demonstration that night in the yard, and I sat on the other side. My lawyer paced back and forth, I told him about Sgt. Rogers, and his similar experience. Mr. Jones apparently discussed this with the lawyer assigned for the state representation.

Sgt. Rogers was ready to testify that DW Lorenzo asked him to watch the same officer that I was watching. His pickup was sabotaged in the same manner that mine was.

Susan looked surprised to see Angel, Dan Romley and Sgt. Rogers at the hearing. Her eyes bugged out when Angel held up the tape she recorded that day in the restaurant.

My hearing came up. I went into the tiny hearing room. Susan sat to the left of the room; I took a seat to the right where Mr. Jones directed me to a seat.

He stood before the judge, Mary Smart, and told my story, very much like he had stated in his office.

Susan denied anything that I 'alleged', and the officiating judge listened. It didn't take her long to rule in my favor.

My daughter, Angel, didn't have to testify.

Neither did Sgt. Rogers, nor Dan Romley.

I was to receive a settlement of $100.000.00.

Relief came, when I knew I wouldn't ever have to 'watch and report' to Susan anymore, but relief really came when I heard in a court of law, that I had won.

That was the reward I wanted.

Thirty five thousand dollars went to Mr. Jones, my lawyer. The remaining amount was all mine.

Six months later I received a letter in the mail from the government. The envelope looked like the IRS envelopes that hold your federal income tax return in the spring of the year.

Inside was a government check for the amount of Forty Two Thousand. A plain sheet of paper with a United States Treasury letter head accompanied the check, it simply stated, 'For Services Rendered.'

The amount was near to my annual payroll. I didn't question it, I just thought of it as being a severance check.

Epilog:

Hale retired with a very nice monthly income. He would need it to keep his promise to Marlow.

The Head of D.O.C., Malcolm Fairchild, resigned. He knew this was a good time to exit.

The warden's assistant/secretary, Marlow Malinski, who gave every kind of sex to whom ever it took to get the best job, is now residing in Gagetown Women's Facility.

She took the rap. She admitted to being behind the break-in and taking my journal. She and one of her cronies, Randy Drake, that's why I heard feet scrambling on the rocks when they escaped. Her reasoning was the journal might reveal her as one of those who were guilty. My notes did tell what the prisoner revealed; merely that it was officers who killed Mayberry.

She had confessed that she was there the day Officer Mayberry was killed, she even confessed to saying, 'kill the bitch'. When Mayberry discovered the group of four, Marlow was having sex with two of them. Marlow refused to tell whom the other two officers were. She convinced the jurors that she didn't have anything to do with Mayberry's murder, and there was insufficient evidence that she killed Kincaid. She is doing 15-30 in the women's prison, in Gagetown Women's Facility.

It was 'scuttle-butt' that some of the female officers were a part of the orgies. Two in particular were Afro-American female officers, who felt intimidated, because of their race and the pressure they were receiving from their superior officers. This was never proven.

Shelia Jones ended up as Marlow's 'roomie' at Gagetown Women's Facility. Shelia realized she had a big mouth. Anyone could have heard what she said at any given time in the visiting room at the prisons. Or she may have made a slip; during conversations she had with family or friends. I was safe, since I never was seen after the dope bust.

DW Susan Lorenzo got what she deserved. Her curiosity revealed what she feared the most, after the day I told her everything. Her husband had fooled everyone, especially her.

Lorenzo did time, fifteen to thirty. Susan divorced him as quickly and quietly as possible. She still is a Deputy Warden.

Godfry in 'I and I' resigned quite suddenly, and now lives out of state. He was a pale-faced skinny man, who, it was reported, suffers from a weak heart.

Andy Gump, Alexander Bartholomew was granted a full pardon by the governor, his record was expunged. This was in exchange for his help to catch the big dope pusher, plus his giving information about the administration's action in Jamestown Prison. He was one of the twelve. He was transferred out the day after he revealed the information about how the dope came in and when it would arrive from Columbia. The agent told him that I was only a pawn, married, with a new life in another state with my husband.

"We all were, weren't we?' Alex asked.

Alex's identity is changed and he is now living with his new wife in Georgia. The state where he visited once when he was a boy, and vowed he'd return someday. He went back to the stone masonry career. I understand the square shaped yellow colored stones there make great fireplaces.

The local agent, Chuck Brimstone, conveniently planted Mary Brown, the secretary's assistant, in the wardens' office. She helped by supplying bits and pieces that she was able to gather from the office.

I am living with my hubby in a remote part of Florida.

He never leaves my side, retiring from truck driving has been good for us both.

I still have nightmares.

My family never did get over the shock of hearing the truth.

Approximately four years after Lorenzo's arrest I read in the paper that Jamestown was scheduled to close down. They started by closing one wing where the convalescents lived. The Feds came in and put an stopple on this action, they added air conditioning, but this didn't work it was not economically feasible, so at present, the prisoners from that wing have been spread and scattered through out the state to several different prisons and that block is closed. The old prison was out-dated. There were lead pipes throughout the penitentiary system, which contributed to the death of many of the prisoners, according to the paper.

Eventually, the prison was closed.

Sgt. Rogers, a true comrade who remained close through many experiences.

Officer Jim Frazier, who was stabbed, with the same shank which went into a prisoner with AIDS, and survived.

He taught me how to bowl, on our prisoner league.

 He was a great officer and friend.

Officer Sam Dwyer, who car-pooled with me, a great officer, with a sense of humor, always kept things light.

Officer Dan Romley, who went to the Academy with me, and stayed supportive throughout my ordeal.

Custody Officer Jim McTaggert, who was educated, and carried a great conversation, without my being bored.

All five had something in common; they shared some of the same experiences as I had. They totaled five of the twelve.

 But they never shared this with me.

Sgt. Rogers' words told it all when he said,

 'You should all be proud of your accomplishments, and being a part of the team.'